Crafts and Craftsmen
of
New Jersey

MORRISTOWN

NEWARK

ELIZABETHTOWN

NEW BRUNSWICK

PRINCETON

MIDDLETOWN

TRENTON

SHREWSBURY

FREEHOLD

BURLINGTON

MOUNT HOLLY

WOODBURY

SALEM

GREENWICH

CAPE MAY

Map of New Jersey, showing population centers of the colonial period

Crafts and Craftsmen
of
New Jersey

Walter Hamilton Van Hoesen

Rutherford • Madison • Teaneck
Fairleigh Dickinson University Press

© 1973 by Associated University Presses, Inc.

Associated University Presses, Inc.
Cranbury, New Jersey 08512

Library of Congress Cataloging in Publication Data

Van Hoesen, Walter Hamilton, 1897-
    Crafts and craftsmen of New Jersey.

    Bibliography: p.
    1. Handicraft—New Jersey—History. 2. Artisans—
New Jersey. 1. Title.
TT24.N5V35   745.5'0949   72-421
ISBN 0-8386-1080-3

Printed in the United States of America

To my mother, from whom I inherited an affection for those things which serve to remind us of the past, and to my wife, who has been most helpful and encouraging in my work.

Contents

Foreword

The history of American arts and crafts has long been neglected by scholars. This is regrettable because the knowledge of a people's furnishings, work implements, decorative arts, and building styles gives us valuable insights into their ways of life. From such data we can learn much about the manner in which individuals worked, worshipped, entertained, established homes, and raised families.

Until recent years no general history of early arts and crafts in New Jersey existed. There were, to be sure, a few useful studies of aspects of the subject. Among these, the most outstanding were Thomas Hopkins and Walter Cox, *Colonial Furniture of West New Jersey* (Haddonfield, N.J., 1936); Julia Sabine, "Silversmiths of New Jersey, 1623-1800," *N.J. Historical Society Proceedings,* LXI, July, 1942; and Carl Williams, *Silversmiths of New Jersey, 1700-1825* (Philadelphia, 1949). It was not until 1964 that the first attempt at a general survey of the subject was made. This was Margaret E. White's *The Decorative Arts of Early New Jersey,* one of the volumes in the New Jersey Bicentennial Historical Series.

Walter Van Hoesen's study represents an important addition to the above literature. He reviews aspects of early craftsmanship and episodes in the lives of the early craftsmen that were not dealt with in the earlier publications. He makes available data that have not been assembled before in so convenient a form.

Van Hoesen's historical materials were accumulated during decades of assiduous searching of the New Jersey countryside for documentation on the early artisans and their artifacts. A professional journalist with a longtime interest in colonial craftsmanship, the author has a rich background for the task he has undertaken. He has written a comprehensive study of the early craftsmen which should be a valuable source for all historians who may wish in the future to investigate the folkways and work patterns of Jerseymen in the eighteenth and early nineteenth centuries.

Willis Rudy

Preface

The place of New Jersey as one of the original thirteen colonies and as a battleground during a large part of the Revolution is well established in history. Through the efforts of numerous writers there has been preserved for posterity a fairly complete record of its beginnings—from a few scattered settlements to the great state that it is today, when its tricentennial has already been observed.

It is a rather surprising fact that comparatively little attention has been paid to the early crafts and craftsmen of New Jersey. The men who worked in the other colonies were given recognition long ago and we are well informed concerning them and their trades. Yet, from the middle of the eighteenth century on, there were cabinetmakers, clockmakers, silversmiths, and other Jerseymen whose skill was such that their work merits high praise, although their identity may not always be known. In the production of pottery and glassware they pioneered.

Extensive research and the gathering of much source material were necessary before undertaking to write about the early days in New Jersey. The trail has led over a long period of years through church and court records, family Bibles, and old newspaper files, as well as county and state histories. In numerous instances it has not been possible to obtain more than a few facts pertinent to a particular subject.

In most instances, I have mentioned in the text a word or two in regard to where I saw a certain piece of furniture, clock, or candlestick. Of course it is impossible to recall years later an authority for statements made back in 1930, when I first got the idea of collecting data on New Jersey's crafts and craftsmen prior to 1830. Over the years I have carried on a vast correspondence with all manner of people, and each time that information concerning a craftsman or his craft has been volunteered, I have jotted it down. Many years as a columnist for the *Newark Sunday News* (1956-1968) were particularly rewarding in that respect. Of course, too, I have done a great deal of reading over the years on all the crafts, and I am the proud possessor of a fine collection of pamphlets that has been especially helpful in this work.

A word of appreciation and acknowledgment is due to various organizations and to a great many people who have assisted so generously with data and advice. The New Jersey Historical Society; the Newark Museum; the New Jersey Society, Sons of the American Revolution; the Holland Society of New York; and members of the Daughters of the American Revolution are mentioned with sincere gratitude. The Monmouth County Historical Society, Burlington County Historical Society, and other groups cheerfully assisted. But most of the individuals who aided are long ago deceased.

Crafts and Craftsmen
of
New Jersey

Historical Background

*I*t always leads to better understanding of a subject (or groups of subjects, as in this case) if first of all a background is sketched. The craftsmen of New Jersey, who labored long and well in the eighteenth and forepart of the nineteenth centuries, were closely identified with historical and economic developments in the State. It is essential to be familiar with the times in which they lived in order fully to appreciate their influence to this day.

No permanent settlements had been established on the land that is now New Jersey until the Swedes set foot on the shores of Delaware Bay. That was in 1638, and for nearly a quarter of a century they sought to colonize the region before surrendering to the Dutch. In Swedesboro and the surrounding countryside we find trace of them, but it is limited mostly to names; very little is known of the lives and customs they followed.

The entire territory had been claimed for the Dutch through discovery by Henry Hudson in 1609, with Fort Orange on the upper North River as one boundary, and another, on the present site of Gloucester, marking the southern limit. The land in between was split into huge tracts, but there was only a handful of men at trading posts and no real effort at colonization.

In 1614 the Dutch had established themselves permanently on Manhattan Island and called it Niew Amsterdam. It was natural that they should cross the river for exploration and to trade with the Indians. The Patroonship of Pavonia was laid out, but about that time the foolish orders of Governor Kieft caused the massacre of many Indians and for years thereafter the territory was hardly safe for white men. When Peter Stuyvesant became governor, he organized a force to drive out the Swedes on the Delaware and sought to make friends with the Indians. It was not until 1660 that a lasting Dutch settlement was founded as the Town of Bergen on the heights, now a part of Jersey City.

Before the English wrested control from the Dutch in 1664, men from the Connecticut colony sought permission to settle in New Jersey, but agreement could not be reached. Hardly had the ships of Charles II anchored in New York Bay before a small band of them landed at a point on the Jersey shore fronting along Staten Island Sound and set up a colony that Sir Philip Carteret named Elizabethtown when he arrived two years later. That was really the beginning of East Jersey.

Carteret had not yet appeared on the scene when Colonel Richard Nicolls, in the name of the Duke of York, started plans for settling the new province. In order to attract New Englanders, he offered them their own town system of control. Within a year after the founding of Elizabethtown, Middletown and Shrewsbury were established on the Monmouth tract. In 1666, with Robert Treat at their head, an entire congregation migrated from New England to the head of what has been known since as Newark Bay, and these people founded the town after which the bay is named.

In the making of plans for Newark, its founders took a step probably unique in the country's Colonial history. In laying out the town site and plotting the main thoroughfares, they set aside what were called tradesmen's lots along Broad Street to be given to the first man of each trade who would settle permanently in the place.

The colonizing work of Nicoll had barely begun to bring results when Carteret and Lord John Berkeley persuaded the Duke of York to grant them a part of the province he had obtained from his king. As a means of getting money they disowned the promise of free town government and decreed that the land must be bought over again or forfeited. The next forty years were one long-continued squabble between the proprietors and colonists and, beyond that, with their heirs, until the Revolution.

Nearly ten years after Carteret landed, the story of West Jersey began. In 1672 he returned to England and Lord Berkeley soon found himself in serious financial difficulties. As a way out of his predicament he sold the western half of New Jersey to two Quakers, John Fenwick and Edward Bellynge. Both became insolvent after a short time and three other Quakers were named trustees. One of them was William Penn, and he was active during the years immediately following in settling boundary disputes and aiding in the first settlement in the region.

Despite his financial reverses Fenwick led the Quakers who formed the vanguard of settlers in New Jersey. With his family, servants, and a company of English, he arrived in Delaware Bay on a single ship in the summer of 1675 and started the colony of Salem. In the autumn of 1677 a second vessel, carrying two hundred and fifty passengers, entered the river and proceeded upstream to the site of Burlington, where another settlement was laid out.

The two colonies flourished, and with the subsequent arrival of other groups, Bridgeton and Greenwich were founded within a few years.

It was in 1682 that the proprietors of East Jersey surrendered their rights to William Penn and his followers for the sum of thirty-four hundred pounds sterling. The same year it was divided into the four counties of Bergen, Essex, Middlesex, and Monmouth.

The colonies of East and West Jersey continued to grow

under Colonial governors until 1702, when they were united and ruled by British crown governors, who also had authority over New York. That continued until, in 1746, the first royal governor for New Jersey was appointed. He and his successors held sway until 1776, when William Franklin, son of Benjamin Franklin and last to hold the office, was arrested and deported to England after two years imprisonment.

The Provincial Congress of New Jersey met in 1776 for the first time at Burlington, Trenton, and New Brunswick in turn to consider the steps to be taken in resisting the authority of England. The following year, on September 20, 1777, the word "colony" was struck from the organic law and the word "state" substituted.

Turning back for a moment to the start of the eighteenth century, we find that a period of steady growth had begun. Colonists from New England continued to move in and settle around Elizabethtown, Newark, and through the counties southward. At the same time English and Dutch families from Long Island crossed over to the Jersey shore around New Brunswick. They spread out into what is now Monmouth County and up the Raritan River into Middlesex, Somerset, and parts of Morris Counties.

The need for labor in glass and iron ventures took large numbers of English, Irish, and other nationalities to the southern part of New Jersey during the early 1700s. The first contingent of Scots arrived at Perth Amboy in 1740 and moved northward to the plains at the foot of the first mountains west of Elizabethtown. A few years later Germans landed at Philadelphia and pushed up the Delaware River before crossing into parts of what are now Hunterdon, Morris, and Warren Counties.

In the late 1760s Moravians who had settled previously at Bethlehem, Pennsylvania, came to New Jersey and founded homes in Warren county. With their arrival the last of the virgin territory within the confines of what is now New Jersey may be said to have become colonized.

Through successive stages of settlement New Jersey had become a fairly prosperous colony by 1770, although the wide differences in the nationality and customs of her people did not make for union. As time went on, the spirit of resistance to British rule manifested itself in some sections, but there was considerable Tory feeling. On the farms living was leisurely and comfortable, even if it was not very profitable, and there was not much excuse for trouble. Finally opposition broke out in determined form and when it was at its height in 1774, citizens of Greenwich, on the Delaware River, staged their own tea party.

By reason of its central position between New York and Philadelphia, the state became the battleground over which a large part of the Revolution was fought from 1775 to 1783, and there are few sections without historical traditions that go back to the war. The population was centered around Elizabethtown, Newark, New Brunswick, Princeton, Trenton, Morristown, Perth Amboy, Burlington, and a few other towns.

During the years of the Revolution armed forces were stationed at many points and foraging parties did extensive damage over wide areas. British troops looted homes and, after driving off the livestock, carried away whatever valuables they could find. In addition, supplies were needed by the Continental Army and the inhabitants found little time to improve their own fortunes. During three winters the Continental forces were quartered in the state.

With the Revolution over in 1783 and the colonies embarked on a course as a nation, New Jersey gradually returned to peaceful pursuits, after almost eight years of continuous fighting. The population grew, water power and mill sites were developed, mining was extended in the northern part of the state, manufacturing started, and a flourishing commerce was carried on by water.

It was before 1800 that New Jersey passed the frontier stage. With large farms dotting most of its area in the south and central portions, mining in the northern part, and business, manufactures, and commerce along the coast, means of travel became essential. Roads were laid out and at each crossroad first a tavern and then a village sprang up. By 1834 the Delaware and Raritan Canal had been completed between New Brunswick and Trenton. Soon afterward the Morris Canal crossed the state further to the north and at the same time the first railroads were being built.

By 1850 New Jersey's place as a leading state in manufactures and other activities had been firmly established. Many enterprises that had started in the smallest way expanded and, particularly in the northern counties, changes took place in rapid succession.

Prior to 1777 there were no newspapers in the colony and the files of those printed earlier in New York and Philadelphia apparently were little used by Jersey craftsmen as an advertising medium. In that year the *New Jersey Gazette* was started in Bridgeton and in 1779 the *New Jersey Journal* made its appearance at Elizabethtown. From that time on, and particularly as other papers were begun, the various publishers found occasional revenue from advertising the wares of clockmakers, silversmiths, and others.

The search for early craftsmen in New Jersey not only ties up with the state's history; it also leads to a better understanding of the part played by its people in the opening of the West. Just as the second and third generations of New England's first settlers had moved into the state, so did Jerseymen play an important part in building up other sections of the country. Even before the nineteenth century they had begun to cross over into Pennsylvania, Ohio, and beyond to find new homes. Today the works of Jersey craftsmen from those years long since past are to be found as family heirlooms in many parts of the country.

One of the earliest and most interesting of the migrations links New Jersey to the Lincoln family. Aside from court records yellowed with age, the only proof of passing is a little headstone on a Monmouth County hillside. Deeds are evidence of the fact that Mordecai Lincoln, great-great-grandfather of Abraham Lincoln, left Massachusetts in 1712, and purchased land not far from Allentown, about fourteen miles out of Trenton.

Mordecai, who was of the third generation of Lincolns in this country from England, may be said to have been one of the state's early craftsmen. He was an ironmaster, or blacksmith. To this day the natives of Crawford's Corners, in Monmouth County, like to point out the supposed site of his shop. He married into the Salter family of that section and acquired considerable land holdings. About 1725 he sold out and moved on to Chester County, Pennsylvania.

John Lincoln, oldest son of Mordecai, tarried in New Jersey for a time and followed the trade of a weaver. Thus he also may be listed as an early craftsman of New Jersey, although there is nothing to which we may point as being the work of either man. Eventually John followed his parent into Pennsylvania and a little later took the next step westward into the Shenandoah Valley.

In New Jersey there remains, besides the deeds, only the grave of Mordecai's little daughter as tangible proof that the Lincolns were here. It is on a knoll called Covell's Hill, scarcely four miles from Allentown, and it is marked by an ancient tombstone that reads:

Deborah

Lincoln

Aged 3 Y 4 M

May 15, 1720

Although in many parts of the state most outward signs of those early days have gone, there are numerous landmarks and places of historical interest that preserve our ties with the past. In places away from the heavily populated areas, where time has not been at work with such a heavy hand, houses are still standing much the same as they were two centuries and more ago, on land that remains in the ownership of descendants of the original settlers. From them it is possible to reconstruct quite accurately a composite picture of life in New Jersey during the colonial and post-colonial days.

2

Early Life and Customs

*A*lmost from the start New Jersey, as one of the so-called middle colonies, became a melting pot for people with differences in blood, religion, language, architecture, and customs. The Swedes and Dutch were in the vanguard. Then came settlers from New England with the Puritan strain and those direct from England, including the Quakers. They were followed by the Scots, Germans, Irish, and other nationalities of Europe.

The influence of the Swedes in New Jersey has not come from those sturdy few who first set foot here. They held sway for a short time over a small area. It was after they had surrendered authority to the Dutch in 1653 that countrymen living across the Delaware River, along the Pennsylvania and Delaware shores, began to migrate eastward in search of new homes and better farm lands. By 1685 they had established themselves over the present Camden, Gloucester, and Salem counties. In 1703 a Swedish church was established on Raccoon Creek and there were a number of flourishing settlements.

Despite the efforts of the Swedes to preserve language and customs, it was a losing fight. The melting pot had begun to work, with the intermarriage of Dutch, English, and other nationalities. Records began to be kept in English and finally, in 1786, the tie with the mother country was broken when existing parishes joined the Episcopal Church. Today scarcely any trace of Swedish life, architecture, or customs are found in South Jersey, and the tradition of those early settlers is kept alive only by the names of families and localities in that region.

The Dutch have maintained their hold on the areas where they first settled, with the result that to this day their influence runs strong along the banks of the Hudson River and in the central counties. The loss of control to the English in 1664 was no barrier to their advancement and they continued to play an important part in the progress of the state. In a search for trace of colonial life and customs in New Jersey, the Dutch are found at every turn.

Most numerous of all, the English settled in practically every section of the state and had a major part in its early development. Each nationality of settlers, however, played a role in the composite picture and contributed a share to the early crafts and arts.

Until the time when the region finally passed into the hands of the English, the Indians who roamed over New Jersey successfully resisted attempts at colonization. Then a better feeling arose and the Leni Lenapes and other red men were induced to sell their land for trinkets, cloth, kettles, and sundry other things. Tracts of land large enough for a town were sometimes sold for a cask of cider.

The Indians were not always entirely satisfied. As the years passed they were crowded more and more until around the middle of the eighteenth century they agreed to an offer from the Legislature to sell all rights, and in return they were settled on a three-thousand-acre tract of land in Burlington County.

In 1801 the few remaining Indians accepted an invitation from the Mohicans in New York to settle on their reservation and after that the remnants of both groups bought land in Michigan. They did not fare well in the west and by 1832 the New Jersey Indians had dwindled to forty members. In that year, sick and poorly kept, they sent an emissary back to New Jersey and he obtained a $2,000 grant from the Legislature for the relinquishing of all claims to land in the state.

That marked the last of the Indians in New Jersey, except for one old brave and his wife, who returned from the Mohican reservation instead of going to Michigan. They settled near Mount Holly in Burlington County and their only child, a daughter, lived in the neighborhood until she died in 1894, past the age of ninety years.

While the Indians influenced the early course of New Jersey, they did not leave any permanent mark and except in a small way took no part in the affairs of those days. Plenty of trace has been found of them, but for the most part it has consisted of arrowheads, fragments of stone weapons, and other articles dug from the ground on old camp sites. Practically nothing has survived of their handicraft.

Although it is a fact given little consideration in history, New Jersey had many slaves, practically from the beginning until as late as 1860. In all of the colonies they were used as laborers on farms and in this state they performed many of the manual tasks around the early glass houses and the forges and furnaces. Thus they were connected in a way with the pioneer crafts of New Jersey.

Berkeley and Carteret attempted to speed the colonizing of New Jersey by encouraging immigrants to bring as many slaves as they could afford. One hundred and fifty acres were offered to every settler, another tract of equal size for each male slave, and seventy-five acres additional for each minor. Later, when they became numerous, the bounty was reduced and then ended altogether.

It is likely that many slaves were brought direct to New Jersey from Africa, because there was established at Perth Amboy, early in the 1700s, a barracks where they were kept when landed from ships until sold. People with the means were not at all averse to owning them. After the establishment of newspapers in the state, they carried advertisements of Negroes to be sold and of rewards for the return of runaways.

Washington's headquarters at Morristown

When in 1777 Washington was in headquarters at Morristown, then a village of several hundred persons in the midst of a farming area, one of his aides wrote to a friend in Elizabethtown telling of a "mulatto girl servant and slave of Mrs. Washington, who eloped, with what design cannot be conjectured" and requested aid in locating her.

The immigrants who came to New Jersey under indenture agreement in colonial times could hardly be called slaves, and yet sometimes they were bought and sold several times before they became free. They have been more aptly called "redemptioners"; they secured passage to America by contracting with the captain of the vessel for their passage. In return the captain had the right to sell such persons. They were obliged to work for a term of years before they were free.

All sorts of people became redemptioners. They included professional men, mechanics, and laborers, who were down in their luck and hoped to get started in a new land. Many of the men who opened up the iron mines in the northern part of the state were redemptioners from Ireland, England, and even Germany. The first glass blowers worked in South Jersey for their freedom after they were brought from Holland and Belgium.

After a time it was unlawful to hold redemptioners for more than four years when they were past seventeen. Their masters were required to give them a start at the end of their terms and a great many of them successfully struck out for themselves after their service was over.

By the middle of the eighteenth century, labor was plentiful enough in the colony so that there was a slackening demand for redemptioners and by the time the Revolution arrived very few of them remained in service. When the war was over they, and a considerable number of the Hessian troops who had fought for the British and had been put to work in the iron mines as captives after being taken prisoner or deserting, settled down as free men to make their homes.

Slavery had lasted until nearly 1800 before the Quakers in the state decided not to own Negroes any longer. As years passed the feeling against slavery increased, until in 1820 the Legislature passed an act for the emancipation of those in servitude. They were not free all at once, but a system of gradual release was adopted by which children obtained freedom when they attained a majority and the aged were cared for as long as they lived. Despite the gradual abolition of slavery, more than six hundred remained in 1840 and even by 1869 there were eighteen.

Education was not attended to as it should have been in

the early years of the colony. The first school of record was in 1664, but it was not until 1693 that the provincial assembly passed an act to "establish schoolmasters for the cultivation of good manners." The schools were not of a very high order and books were very scarce. As living conditions improved, the authorities of the various towns contracted for men of learning to teach their children, but it was a long time before schoolhouses appeared in rural sections.

The College of New Jersey was founded at Elizabethtown in 1746, with the Reverend Mr. Dickinson as the first president and only instructor. At his death about a year later the college was removed to Newark, where the Reverend Aaron Burr, father of Aaron Burr of Revolutionary fame, became president. Ten years later it was transferred to Princeton, which was then a mere hamlet. In the Revolution the main college building, Nassau Hall, played a part in the Battle of Princeton and was a temporary meeting place for the Continental Congress when it was forced to leave Philadelphia.

Doctors were almost as slow in coming into prominence as schoolmasters. In fact, women were the first to care for the sick. As the population grew, physicians became more numerous, and in 1766 the first medical association was formed. Doctors came to be influential in their communities and performed many other services in addition to attending the afflicted.

Bearing in mind the different nationalities that went to make up the settlers in New Jersey, it is interesting to consider the various' styles of architecture from the early colonial period. The Dutch and others who followed them in the northern part of the state took largely to the use of stone in building their houses and the first structures were set partly into the ground. Later they were raised to a story and a half, with the upper part sometimes of wood. Still later, they became the kitchen when the main body of the house was built, with the familiar gambrel roof in the front and rear. The old stone walls were well over two feet thick, but unfortunately they were laid up in clay mortar, lime mortar being used only on the outer side. Time and weather loosened the joints and caused many a place to fall into ruin.

In Melick's admirable *Story of An Old Farm* there is to be found a splendid description of the stone houses as they were in the eighteenth century. He recounts the threshold as being guarded by a double Dutch door. Small windows were set deep in thick walls for warmth in winter and coolness in summer. Says Melick:

In some of the houses the best rooms were wainscoted in oak and red cedar, but in most instances they were just whitewashed. No carpets were to be seen, but floors were covered with silver sand done into fanciful figures by a broom.

The living room, or kitchen, served many purposes in those days and it was there that life centered. With the exception of what was baked in the outer Dutch oven, cooking was done before a huge fireplace, around which hung warming pans, flat irons, skillets, teapots and other necessary articles. From the chimney's spacious throat were suspended cranes, hooks, pots, trammels and smokejacks.

Lofty chests of drawers and cupboards extending nearly to the ceiling were the principal pieces of furniture. On the Dutch dresser of massive proportions were displayed polished porringers, plates of pewter and sometimes wooden trenchers. There were no closets and household articles were hung about the walls or on pegs from the beams. In a corner mortars were kept for powdering mustard or coffee and other work, while the family Bible and a tinder box were on a corner shelf for daily use.

Most of the space in the upper chambers was taken up by four-poster beds and clothing was kept either in a large press, or hung on pegs from the rafters. Frequently sleeping quarters were in one corner of the main room downstairs and it was only with the coming of more prosperous years that the second floor was utilized for anything other than storage.

The houses built in North Jersey after 1800 were marked by the influence of the settlers moving in from New England. Georgian columns, more elaborate doorways, fanlights, and other of the finer architectural details peculiar to the English were adopted, while here and there a dwelling was erected typical throughout of British origin. Wood was adopted more generally and for warmth the walls were filled with brick or stone.

The styles of colonial houses in northern and southern New Jersey were different in numerous respects. In the extreme southern portion of the state, where the Swedes had held sway for a short period, the Dutch architecture took on some of the Swedish tendency and over the rest of the region the English exerted an important influence.

In the southern counties the earliest buildings were made of logs. One of the few such structures that have survived is hidden away on a back road near Four Miles, Burlington County, and dates from around 1720.

It was only a short time before advantage was taken of the clay and sandy soil and houses were built of native brick. At first they were one story, with gambrel roofs; later a second floor was added where the attic used to be. The age of many of these old dwellings is fixed by dates worked into the brick by the builders.

In towns along the Jersey coast and here and there over the countryside the more affluent settlers were able gradually to erect quite pretentious houses. They imported both materials and skilled artisians to do the work. Glazed brick from Holland was used to make the fireplaces, while hand-blocked wallpaper was brought over from England and France. Even prior to the Revolution, life had become rather leisurely for a small part of the population. Considerable style was maintained by the leading families in Elizabethtown, New Brunswick, Burlington, and a few other places.

Records of the colonial era reveal that the average Jerseyman enjoyed comparatively few luxuries. Except among the well-to-do, chinaware was scarce and rarely exceeded more than a dozen pieces in a household. In a few homes such necessities as cups, saucers, and bowls were of Delft or Queensware. More often these articles, and plates, servers, platters, spoons, pots, and tankards were of wood, iron, copper, or pewter. There was little glassware in use and silverware was restricted for the most part to a few tablespoons or teaspoons in the household.

In furniture, mahogany was the most costly and within the means of only a few. Almost every family had dressers, corner cupboards, and a few chairs or stools, and one or two beds. Usually these were made of bilstend, also called gumwood, or pine, walnut, cherry, or red cedar, although occasionally other native woods were used. Pieces in daily use were seldom of other than rough home make and those of more expert craftsmanship were choice posessions.

In colonial New Jersey men traded by barter, and free land was a bait to attract settlers. Money was seldom seen and roads were almost nonexistent. The settlers were not particularly prosperous and the worldly goods they brought with them were limited. Furthermore, they were obliged to rely in large part on trade with New York or Philadelphia, and taxes levied by those places on incoming goods were a handicap. Cloth and garments for the family were made by the women, while the menfolk cleared their land for farming and fashioned their own furniture and tools.

Gradually villages on streams attracted mills. By 1800 there were 1100 in the state, of which nearly half were gristmills and the remainder either sawmills or operated in conjunction with forges, furnaces, or other enterprises. The mining of iron and iron manufacture became leading industries, although ceramics, glassmaking, and other activities shared the picture.

Although industry had its start far back in the state's history, New Jersey's fertile soil has always made agriculture foremost in certain sections. The earliest records of the Dutch on Manhattan Island tell of the "bouerie," or gardens on the west bank of the Hudson, the fields of grain, thriving cattle, and poultry. During the brief period when Swedish farmers tilled their acres in the lower Delaware River valley, they produced their own rye, tobacco, and flax before the Dutch took over. Later English settlers brought livestock and varieties of garden plants.

Before the nineteenth century New Jersey was exporting beef, horses, pork, flour, and other products. At one time Hunterdon County was the best wheat-raising area in America. Gradually, as the West opened up, the state lost in agricultural importance, but it has continued to support a substantial farming gentry.

3

Jersey Cabinetmakers

J ust when the first cabinetmakers worked in New
Jersey must remain a matter of conjecture. The early
colonists brought with them only the barest necessities for
starting life in a new land and undoubtedly many of them
were obliged to turn a hand in fashioning articles of furniture for their own homes. As the reputations of some of
them grew, it seems reasonable to assume that their services
were in demand, but if any pieces from those earliest days
survive, the absence of labels or other markings prevents
identification.

Records of the latter part of the seventeenth and beginning of the eighteenth centuries would indicate that Jerseymen depended in large part on the craftsmen of New York
and Philadelphia and those from New England for most
of their needs. As a matter of fact, this continued to be true
right through the colonial period. Much of the handiwork
thought to be of local origin because of inheritance from
generation to generation came from outside the state.

It was not until after the middle of the eighteenth century that cabinetmakers began to establish themselves in
various parts of the colony. Even then the way was not easy
for them, and local history reveals that they were carpenters,
makers of coffins when occasion required, or were useful in

other ways to eke out a living. In a few instances they were native sons who returned from New York or Philadelphia after learning the trade, but in the main they were craftsmen from those cities or more distant places seeking to better their lot.

Even early in the present century Jerseymen seldom got into Newark, Elizabeth, or other population centers of the state, to say nothing of New York and Philadelphia. In earlier times they had to be content with occasional trips for necessities over dirt roads or paths to towns that were usually county seats. Mostly they were self-sufficient and it is logical that so-called rural furniture came into use.

Rural furniture is not the same as country furniture, which was made in towns and cities for people who lived in the country and possessed the means to pay for it. Rural

Jersey farmhouse pine table

Jersey rural dresser

furniture was made closer to home, in a manner of speaking
—on the farm or in the village shop. In any event it was
made for the most part by craftsmen. They had skill and
a pretty good idea of local needs.

In some instances they were natives who had gone to the
city and learned furniture making by becoming apprenticed
to established artisans. On other occasions they had been
city dwellers who chose to live closer to the land and were
already possessed of expertise when they arrived.

It did not take long for word to spread over the countryside when a farmer, blacksmith, or general storekeeper was
able to make chests, corner cupboards, and other furniture
in his spare time. Only such things as a cradle for the first
born, a chest or tool box for one's own use, or a table for
temporary service were made on the spot. True, chairs and

Pine breakfront cupboard

other furniture in need of emergency attention were kept
in repair, but they had been made originally by craftsmen
in the area.

A desk-on-frame found in the Cornell house in Penning-
ton, built about 1705, is an example of early rural furniture

in New Jersey. Made of native walnut, it is mainly Queen Anne style, but with spindle turned legs ending in ball feet.

New Jersey's cabinetmakers are not to be credited with originality of design. Like other successful tradesmen they chose to please their customers and executed pieces after any of the favored styles. Thus we find huge cupboards reaching from floor to ceiling made for the Dutch families of Monmouth and Bergen counties, while the English in the southern counties and around Elizabethtown favored adaptations of the Hepplewhite or Sheraton styles.

Shipping records of New Brunswick, Perth Amboy, and other ports that flourished along the Jersey shore during the colonial period reveal that some furniture made in New Jersey was carried to Savannah, Charleston, and other parts of the South, but that most of the trade was monopolized

Combination washstand and dresser

Old cherry wardrobe

by the New England craftsmen. Incoming vessels bore mahogany from San Domingo and much of it went into yards catering to cabinetmakers. Other items occasionally appearing were hardware, brasses, and inlay material.

Although mahogany was in quite general use in towns along the coast, the craftsmen who worked inland apparently found it more convenient and less expensive to utilize native woods, for the supply, as well as the variety, was abundant. Cherry, cedar and walnut were favorites. Others were chestnut, maple, hickory, ash, and even apple.

In the forefront of New Jersey cabinetmakers were the Mathew Egertons, father and son, who worked for more than half a century in New Brunswick. The elder man was born in 1739. He established himself in the trade prior to the Revolution and in 1785 was joined by his son.

A South Jersey four-poster bed

The Egertons were contemporaries of that period when other leading craftsmen included the Townsends and Goddards in New England and William Savery of Philadelphia. Then, too, there was Duncan Phyfe, who is identified with New Jersey, notwithstanding that his shop was in New York City. Undoubtedly Phyfe was acquainted with both of the Egertons, because family interests in his later years took him for extended periods to within a few miles of New Brunswick.

In 1785 Mathew Egerton, who had served in the Revolution, and his son were in business together, with a shop that is still standing in Burnet Street, New Brunswick, a short distance from the Raritan River. It is of brick construction, three stories high, and in the rear is the warehouse where he displayed his furniture. The property has deteriorated with the years and has been unoccupied for many years.

The house long-occupied by the younger Egerton is located at 72 Schurman Street, a few blocks from Burnet Street. A small frame dwelling, it is practically hidden by a structure erected directly in front of it.

From advertisements in newspapers of the period in connection with the settling of his estate, it is known that Mathew Egerton, Sr., died in 1802. From then on until 1837 when he, too, passed on, the younger man continued to serve a large clientele that included many of the foremost

Eighteenth-century tall chest. COURTESY RICHARD C. GAINE

Eighteenth-century side tables

families in the central part of the state. He became active in civic affairs and from 1790 to 1800 was one of the vestrymen of Christ Episcopal Church. In 1822 he was second vice-president of the New Jersey Bank for Savings in New Brunswick and was listed as the owner of considerable property in the town.

There is no furniture definitely attributable to the elder Egerton by means of labels. It is known that he was a successful cabinetmaker for years. His ability is attested by the knowledge of the craft imparted to his son and reflected in the authentic pieces of the younger man.

Two things lead to the conclusion that the elder Egerton did not follow the practice of identifying his work. For one thing, the labeled pieces without the "Jr." so far brought to light appear to be from years after his death, while those with it are from the earlier period. An inventory of his shop listed in an advertisement in the *New Brunswick Advertiser* of September 2, 1803, to close out his estate mentions "a complete set of cabinetmaker's tools of every description; a large stock of excellent seasoned stuff, consisting of mahogany, cherry, black walnut and gumwood boards, a small pile of chestnut rails and some very valuable household furniture."

Mathew Egerton, Junior, label

Mathew Egerton, Jr., is reliably credited with using two different labels during his lifetime. The first was octagonal in shape, similar to the one illustrated, which was found on the case of a Leslie & Williams tall clock made for Colonel Charles Morgan of Marlboro Township in Monmouth County. In addition to a place for indicating the number of the piece, this style of label has the suffix "Junior," which supports the theory that it was used during his father's lifetime.

Egerton label on Leslie & Williams tall clock

The second label is oval in design and has the name without any suffix. The address is shown as Burnet Street, New Brunswick, and it is known that he continued there after his father's death. It has been found on delicately executed pieces of Hepplewhite and Empire periods when Egerton, Jr., was conducting the business by himself.

Egerton, Jr., married Myria Bergen, member of an old Middlesex County family. They had two sons, John and Evert, both of whom learned the cabinetmaker's trade. John was in business for himself and worked at other occupations, but Evert went into his father's shop and after 1825 the firm was known as Egerton & Son. Old records tell of a cyclone that descended upon New Brunswick in

Dutch kas by Mathew Egerton, Jr. COURTESY RICHARD C. GAINE

1835, and refer to the considerable damage done to the Egerton dwelling and adjoining warehouse in Burnet Street.

The handiwork of Mathew Egerton, Jr., is preserved in more than a score of known Dutch cupboards or kases, secretaries, gracefully executed tall clock cases, and other pieces with the original labels fastened to them. A majority of these pieces are in the hands of descendants of the original purchasers. His mastery of his art is attested by comparing the huge and solidly constructed sideboards with the delicately but finely proportioned tables and secretaries.

Egerton, Jr., was representative of the best ability among American cabinetmakers during the eras when Chippendale, Sheraton, Hepplewhite, and early Empire stylings were popular. Much of his work shows the beautiful characteristic inlay. Except for the kas, usually made in cherry with walnut moldings, he preferred mahogany for most of his furniture.

In some of the Egerton pieces there is evidence of rare skill in combining the best of designs from abroad. This was true of sewing and side tables, with Sheraton top and legs, after the Empire style. Bureaus of the Hepplewhite period were made with a deep top drawer, often hinged and fitted with pigeonholes, to serve as a desk. The several authenticated Hepplewhite-style sideboards are most excellent examples of craftsmanship in all its branches and in this writer's judgment are a key to the identity of the maker of similar pieces that have been found in the Dutch country along the Hudson River.

At the time of his death the stock of furniture on hand in Egerton's showroom consisted of four bureaus priced from $25 to $35 each, a bookcase at $50, a pair of end tables at $25, a workstand at $13, two pine dressing tables at $10 and $3, and a cherry bureau at $10.

Another New Brunswick cabinetmaker was John Ryckman, who advertised on May 6, 1793, that he had lately removed from New York and located at the upper end of Albany Street.

Egerton clothes press

An eighteenth-century dresser

Chippendale-style washstand

I have referred previously to Duncan Phyfe and stated that he was identified with New Jersey. When he came to this country from Scotland in 1783, as a lad of sixteen years, his family first settled in Albany, where he learned his trade in his father's shop. Ten years later he removed to New York and started business in Partition (now Fulton) Street and it was there that he gained success as furniture maker to the city's leading citizens.

In 1814, when Phyfe was nearing the height of his career, he found time to turn architect and even to aid in the construction of a house for his daughter, Eliza, who moved into it as a bride. That house is standing today amid towering trees fully as old as itself on the main street of New Market, in Middlesex County. It is owned by a religious order.

Empire period sofa

Undoubtedly the most interesting feature of the house is the initials "D. P." apparently scratched with a diamond on a pane in a rear window of the first floor. Handwriting experts have attested that they are those of Duncan Phyfe. The angle of the letters and the general formation are identical with those of his signature.

When the property was sold in 1920 by descendants of William Vail, who married Phyfe's daughter, a one-story building stood under the trees on a broad expanse of lawn. It was Phyfe's private workshop, although there is no record of what he made there, and on the walls were remains of the racks that held his tools. The space between ceiling and roof was cluttered with pieces of mahogany and other woods, undoubtedly left over from furniture that he had made and placed there to serve as insulation.

The Phyfe house, as it is known, is unusual in many

architectural details. It is a part of local history that he
spent much time there with his daughter, particularly after
his retirement in 1847, until he died six years later.

Among the early cabinetmakers of Trenton was William
Kerwood. An advertisement that appeared in *The State
Gazette* in 1808 referred also to Samuel Moon, a Windsor
chairmaker, with whom he had a working agreement. The
notice follows:

> William Kerwood, cabinet and chairmaker, Trenton, opposite
> The Market House, returns his thanks to the public for the share
> of patronage he has hitherto enjoyed and solicits a continuance of
> it, and no endeavours shall be wanting on his part to give complete
> satisfaction to all his customers. He also keeps for sale at his rooms
> Windsor chairs, manufactured by Samuel Moon, near Morris-
> ville. The general applause Mr. Moon's work has met with
> makes any recommendation of it unnecessary.

Ichabod Williams is credited with being a cabinetmaker
in Elizabethtown, where he was born May 10, 1768, the
son of Thomas Williams. He is supposed to have learned
his trade in New York and later opened a shop in Water
Street (now Elizabeth Avenue). He had a large clientele
among his fellow townsmen for many years and is known
to have made cases for the tall clocks of his brother-in-law,
Aaron Lane, although labels have not been found to identify
his work. Following his death on September 23, 1837, he
was buried in the yard of the First Presbyterian Church on
Broad Street, Elizabeth.

In 1897 the firm of Rousett & Mulford carried on the
Elizabethtown Cabinet Warehouse. A notice in the *New
Jersey Journal* of March 27 in that year, and also found on
clock cases and furniture, reads:

> Elizabethtown Cabinet Warehouse, Rousett & Mulford, cabinet-
> makers, near the stonebridge, in Elizabethtown, intend keeping
> for sale a handsome variety of fashionable furniture, which they
> have determined to sell low for cash or produce.
>
> Abraham Rousett
Abraham Mulford
>
> Mahogany for sale, apply above

Abraham Rousett, who formed the partnership with Abraham Mulford in the early 1800s, had been a cabinetmaker. Born in 1780, he was a son of David Rousett, who was a leather dresser and also kept a tavern on Second River, now the Bellville section of Newark.

The first notice of Abraham Rousett as a cabinetmaker appeared in the *Federal Republican* for December 6, 1803. After serving an apprenticeship in New York, he had removed that year to Elizabethtown seeking to escape a yellow fever epidemic. The first page of the same paper for December 13, 1803, carried a second notice directly underneath a wood cut showing a tall-case clock, a table and cradle, two stools, and a coffin. It read: "Cabinet Furniture of every description may be had on the shortest notice and most reasonable terms, by applying to the subscriber, near the stone Bridge."

A notice in February of the following year was in a humorous vein, as follows: "To brag or not to brag—that is the question. Whether it is nobler to be passive and patient, wait the calls of custom, or swell the columns of a newspaper with feats of workmanship beyond compare."

The same year Rousett was accepting orders on behalf of Samuel Thompson, coppersmith and tin plate worker on Water Street, New York, according to newspaper cards sponsored by Thompson.

Rousett's final notice in March, 1810, was an announcement of public sale, as follows:

To be sold at Public Vendue, on Thursday, the 29th inst., at 2 o'clock P.M., at the shop lately occupied by Mr. Rousett, near the Stone Bridge, in Elizabethtown, new furniture—

Bureaus, Tables, Clothespress, Cradles and other articles partly finished. Mahogany boards, planks, joices, veneering, etc. Cherry, Black Walnut, Gum, Whitewood and Pine boards, Maple Joice. Work Benches, Tools, tin plates, Stoves, etc.—Also, the large workshop, two stories high, with the back building—an excellent stand for a Storekeeper or Mechanic.

A headstone in the First Presbyterian churchyard reads: "In memory of Abraham Rousett, who died April 8, 1815, in the 35th year of his age."

The first notices of Rousett's partnership with Abraham Marsh Mulford appeared in papers during March, 1807. The woodcut at the top of notices showed a cradle and a coffin enclosed in a square, with an appeal for apprentices. Sandwiched between was the announcement that "Rousett & Mulford, cabinet-makers, near the Stone Bridge, in Elizabethtown, intend keeping for sale a handsome variety of cabinet furniture."

The partnership was dissolved in March, 1808. Rousett continued at the old stand until 1810, when he gave up business, as indicated by the above-quoted notice of sale. Mulford opened a lumber yard and mill on the Elizabeth River, off of present-day West Grand Street. Successive generations carried on the business until the last of the line died several years ago.

Although the firm of Rousett & Mulford was in business a short time, its warehouse was the first in New Jersey to display products of its own shop and those of other craftsmen. The cases of several tall clocks known to have come from their place are not labeled, but they are identical with those made by John Scudder.

John Scudder was a cabinetmaker in the Rahway-Westfield area during the late 1700s and into the early years of the next century before leaving for Ohio in 1815. According to a family Bible in possession of a direct descendant, he was born October 10, 1770. Town records, the public library, and the Presbyterian Church in Westfield combine to give quite a complete picture of him. There were two other Scudders with the same name during the same period, but careful research has established that they were in different branches of the family and followed other careers.

The cabinetmaker was a nephew of Benjamin, a carpenter and wheelwright, from whom he apparently learned his craft. Benjamin had a large farm and several mills along the Rahway River near Springfield. He made marginal notes each day for years on calendar almanacs that are now in the special collections section at Rutgers University Library.

The earliest known record of John's work as a cabinetmaker is a hand-written inscription on the label of a tall clock reading: "June the 5th, 1793. Made by John Scudder, Jr., a cabinetmaker in Westfield." The clock was sold in 1959 at a New York gallery, and label and inscription were copied at that time, but the present owner is not known.

An undated tax list of Westfield residents during the 1790s shows John Scudder, Jr., a single man owning neither land nor livestock. Apparently he was subject to taxes as a cabinetmaker. Westfield Presbyterian Church records reveal his marriage on January 29, 1794, to Chloe Sayre, daughter of Mathias Sayre. According to the before-mentioned tax list, Sayre kept a tavern on the Westfield-Elizabeth road.

On July 26, 1795, Scudder is recorded as having been baptized with a son, Caleb. In 1800 both John and Chloe Scudder were listed as church communicant members. Baptismal records show three more children, the last in 1809. In September, 1810, Chloe, aged 32 years, was buried from the church.

The next year John married Susanna Miller, whose sister, Rebecca, married John, son of Isaac Brokaw, then a clockmaker in Rahway. She was the daughter of Andrew and Sarah Ross Miller, also of Westfield. Two daughters by his second marriage and the wedding of his son, Caleb, in August, 1814, precede the unpublished minutes of the church for July 25, 1815, which end with the brief statement:

"The clerk reported that John Scudder and his wife were dismissed to put themselves under the care of some Presbyterian church in Ohio."

One of the first Jersey cabinetmakers to identify his work, Scudder used a label without an address. He is known, however, to have lived and to have had his shop on the road leading to Rahway. He cut his name on some work, after which he seared it with a red-hot piece of metal. Chests have been found so branded. He is known, also, to have made tall clock cases for the Brokaws in Rahway and for Joachim Hill, near Flemington, until his erstwhile apprentice, James Topping, took over.

In the first issue of the *Bridgetown* (Rahway) *Museum* and *New Jersey Advertiser,* dated July 13, 1822, one of the notices listed Meeker & Clarkson as purveyors of fine furniture. They are shown as cabinetmakers, but no further clue has been found as to their activities.

Town records of Chester, Morris County, reveal that James Topping, a cabinetmaker, was one of the earliest settlers in that community. He purchased twelve acres of woodland from David Welsh in December, 1820, and in 1829 he bought a house that had been built by an Isaac Corwin. In after years he added to the structure. His last survivor was a daughter who died in 1939, and the following year the dwelling was sold to settle the estate.

The accounts of Topping show that he made various articles of furniture for families inhabiting the Morris County countryside, but none of it has been positively identified. He was apprenticed to John Scudder of Westfield in 1795 when he was only fifteen years old, according to family history. Born in 1780, he became prominent and conducted many activities until death in 1874 at the advanced age of ninety-four years.

Topping entered the Scudder household during the closing years of the eighteenth century and in 1802 he married a Westfield girl named Sarah Marsh, soon after the purchase of land from his employer. According to a deed on file in Essex county (Union was not set aside until 1856) it was described as "a plantation of ground on the road from Springfield to Scotch Plains" and Richard Van Kirk of Westfield was a partner in the venture.

After seven years' apprenticeship, Topping was just ending his training period at the time of his marriage and realty undertaking. Nothing has come to light thus far regarding

Van Kirk, who also was an apprentice under Scudder, but it is my belief that he was a member of a family by that name then living in Elizabeth.

Within a year Topping sold his interest back to Scudder and ended his affiliation with Westfield by returning to Chester. He lived for years in a house on Main Street, with a shop "nearly opposite." He introduced the first spring wagon in the area and made such vehicles, as well as furniture, for neighboring farmers.

The Isaac Corwin house mentioned before is still standing at the intersection of present-day Route 206 and Main Street. It is now operated as Larison's Turkey Farm. The two back rooms were used by Topping for his shop to make furniture.

Prominent among the cabinetmakers in Newark during colonial times was Robert Nichols. He was a man of various other attainments and the father of a large family. His house and adjoining shop were located on what is now Washington Street, where he catered to the needs of his fellow townsmen, beginning about 1760, until 1790.

An account book kept by Nichols reveals that, like many other craftsmen of his day, he was not against turning his hand to any work to bolster his income and that "the boys in the shop" were his assistants in all undertakings. One entry in 1763 was for a bed frame, another for a coffin for which he charged 1.1.9, and a third noted a day's labor for all hands in the harvest fields. In that same year he made Venetian blinds for the mansion of Elias Boudinot on Broad Street, Newark, and on various occasions repaired the town dock.

Although no furniture has been found that may be definitely attributed to them, Mathias and Caleb Bruen are known to have been cabinetmakers in Newark from Revolutionary War days until sometime in the nineteenth century. A map of Broad Street in 1796 shows that they had a shop in that year on the thoroughfare, a little west of Hill Street. They were descendants of Obadiah Bruen, who was one of the early settlers. A brother of Mathias and Caleb was a shoemaker, and his shop was on the corner of Broad and Hill Streets. The Bruen homestead was next to the cabinet-making establishment.

A cabinet and furniture maker prominently identified with the colonial history of New Jersey, although it cannot be said with certainty that he followed the trade in this state, was Benjamin Randolph. The earliest record of him is in Philadelphia, where he appears to have been a woodworker in 1768. As such he worked on the interior of a number of structures, including a new almshouse erected in that year.

In 1770 Randolph apparently was a maker of wooden buttons, with a shop on Chestnut Street, Philadelphia, and a little later he advertised as a chairmaker "at the Sign of the Golden Eagle" on the same thoroughfare. It was here that Thomas Jefferson stopped on his first visit to Philadelphia in 1775.

Randolph was a member of the Philadelphia City Troop and took part with his company in the Battles of Trenton and Princeton. The *Philadelphia Evening Post* for May 6, 1777, carried an advertisement inserted by him seeking to purchase firearms for the Continental forces. Later in the same year he moved to Burlington County in New Jersey, and settled at Chatsworth to manage the Speedwell furnace, which he purchased from Daniel Randolph, a brother. He lived there until his death in 1791, and in his will left the property to a daughter.

Most of Randolph's furniture was made in Philadelphia prior to the Revolution. One of the pieces identified as his is the portable writing desk on which Thomas Jefferson wrote the draft of the Declaration of Independence and he is said also to have made the boxes in which the papers of the Continental Congress were kept. Three chairs identified as having been made by Randolph have sold at auction for $33,000, $15,000, and $9,000. The pieces of furniture mentioned are considered among the best examples of colonial craftsmanship and it may well be that in the quiet years after operating the Speedwell furnace he was occupied at least a part of his time at his original trade.

One of the early nineteenth-century cabinetmakers in Burlington was Thomas Aikman, member of a God-fearing family of Scotch Presbyterians who first settled in the town about 1702. Records of old St. Mary's Church indicate that he was active in its affairs for more than forty years, beginning in 1800.

No labels to identify Aikman's work have been found, but pieces of furniture cherished to this day by families in and around Burlington are credited to him. The registry of St. Mary's shows that he married Jane Lazelere on October 7, 1802. The baptism of Hannah Jane, a daughter, on December 22, 1816, and the death of Aikman's wife on May 21, 1818, are recorded.

In 1819 Aikman was treasurer of St. Mary's Church, then for many years its clerk. It is related that he led the singing and frequently displayed the disposition and singleness of purpose of his ancestors.

Abraham Clark, one of New Jersey's signers of the Declaration of Independence, turned to cabinetmaking to fill the need for furniture in his own home. A chair with his initials cut in the underside of the seat, and a desk in the possession of descendants, give evidence of his ability.

Born at Elizabethtown on February 16, 1726, Clark was the son of an alderman and belonged to a family prominent in the early days of the colony. Educated as a farmer, he showed early signs of ability for public service. He started his career as sheriff of what was then Essex County. When the Revolution began he was one of the most active patriots and, as a member of the Continental Congress and in other positions, served his country until death resulted from a sun stroke in 1794.

Without education for the law, Clark's willingness to help people in need earned him the title of "poor man's lawyer." His home for many years was on the outskirts of Rahway, and he is buried in the old cemetery that faces on St.

George's Avenue, where his tombstone inscription bears evidence of the regard in which he was held by his neighbors.

The early settlers of the Black River country, where the hills of northern Somerset County merge with those of Hunterdon and Morris, turned to William Willets when they needed furniture. His father, Cornelius, was the pioneer in that region and around the 1760s built the first mill, where wheat was ground during the Revolution to help feed Washington's army at Morristown. Prior to 1800 it was sold to John Potter, after whom the locality came to be called Pottersville.

It was on the Pottersville-Lamington road, which skirts the south branch of the Raritan River, that William Willets ran a combined blacksmith and cabinet shop from soon after the Revolution until later than 1810. His great-granddaughter, Mrs. Ida Vliet Alpaugh, lived on the site of the shop until her death in 1950 at the age of ninety-one years. At her death she had a curly maple secretary, table, and other pieces made by him. Willets, like most other cabinetmakers, did not devote all of his time to the trade but worked in it along with his blacksmithing. The wood he used was cut from nearby hills and was seasoned in anticipation of orders.

No labeled pieces have been found to make certain identification of Willets's work, but some furniture in the possession of families now living in the region has been inherited, along with the tradition that he was the maker.

An outstanding cabinetmaker in Paterson during the forepart of the 1800s was Christopher Van Pelt. Louis Beach Vreeland, a native of that city and later of Charlotte, North Carolina, gave me before he died in 1965 the details concerning his great-grandfather.

Young Van Pelt was apprenticed to the machinist trade and worked for a time in Paterson shops, where the nation's first steam engines were made, but his skill as a cabinetmaker was greater, especially after he was taken into the Vreeland family and married one of their womenfolk. One of his tall case clocks is in the Winterthur Museum at Wilmington, Delaware; another was among the prized possessions of Mr. Vreeland. Van Pelt also made a secretary-dresser, shaving stand, chairs, children's stools, and ornamental boxes, all of which are family heirlooms.

William Abell moved from Goshen, New York, to Elizabeth in 1820 and carried on the cabinetmaker's trade until his death. He is buried in the old cemetery of Connecticut Farms, near Route 22, in Union. Among his known pieces is a modified Governor Winthrop-style desk. It is of cherry wood, with twelve expertly made little drawers instead of the usual pigeonholes. The hardware is of beehive design.

A descendant has the Abell account book, started at Goshen in 1817. While in Elizabeth, it shows, he made tables, coffins, ploughs, wagon whiffletrees, chairs, and other articles. She also has his drawing instruments, pocketbook, and rat-tail silver flatware.

A lady living in Far Hills several years ago wrote me an interesting story concerning a desk made by a probable Jerseyman named George S. Woodruff. Her letter reads:

> We are lucky enough to find an old country pine desk made in a unique style and in need of repairs and yet definitely salvagable. We left the old buttermilk paint on the inside of the secretary part and on the underside of the slant top. Under the red paint we found a notation "Made by George S. Woodruff, Washington, D. C., died 1861 20 years, less 20 days."
>
> Another notation where the slant top lifts up reads "made by George S. Woodruff, Washington, D. C." followed by "Dear Mother, I take my pen in hand to write to you."

My correspondent theorized that the young man may have been killed in the Civil War and had previously sent the desk to his parents in New Jersey.

John Mann was a cabinetmaker working in the Elizabethtown-Newark area between 1792-1800, according to newspaper cards of the time. Apparently he followed in the footsteps of his grandfather, Joseph, a single mention of whom is found in the record in 1739, when he was a justice of the peace. At the same time he was a carpenter, referred to in the setttlement of Ebenezer Lyon's estate as "the Justice mun who furnished a coffin."

John was christened in St. John's Episcopal Church, Elizabethtown, in December, 1770. First public announcement of his work came in May, 1792, when the *Newark Gazette & Commercial Advertiser* carried a notice over the name Gray & Mann reading:

> The subscribers take this method of informing the public that in consequence of frequent solicitations, they have taken the shop opposite Mr. Sayre's tavern, where they intend carrying on business. From their endeavors to give general satisfaction to those who shall favor them with their command, they flatter themselves that they will meet with encouragement from the liberal public, which shall ever be esteemed as particular favor by their most obedient humble servants.

The same paper, the following July, announced "the marriage of John Mann of Newark to Miss Sally Hinds of Rahway, by the Reverend Woodruff." In June, 1793, he signed a mortgage to Elisha Boudinot of Newark for 120 pounds sterling. The same month Gray & Mann announced an end to their partnership and Elisha Boudinot sold to Mann, for the same amount as his mortgage, the property in Newark on which Mann continued as a cabinet-maker until 1795, when he removed to Elizabethtown.

The *New Jersey Journal* for January 11, 1797, carried the following terse request over his name, with the Elizabethtown address:

> All persons indebted to the subscriber are requested to call and discharge their accounts prior to the 23rd instant.

On November 20, 1798, the same paper carried the following:

> The subscriber wishes to inform the public that he is engaged in the Cabinet Making Business, next door to the Printing Office, where any person may be supplied with anything they need in that line on a short notice.

Apparently Mann moved to Rahway in the early 1800s, because St. John's Church records for April 26, 1807, list two children as having been christened and their birth date in Rahway as November 6, 1866. During the next decade, as a judge in the Essex County courts, he witnessed wills, settled estates, and performed other judicial services for residents of Elizabethtown, Rahway, Clark, Westfield, and Scotch Plains. His death was reported on May 1, 1831.

Richardson Gray was one of the Gray & Mann partnership. Born in Elizabethtown in 1754, he is noted in the records of St. John's Episcopal Church, that city, as having been christened, with two brothers, in 1760.

Gray made cases for some of the Isaac Brokaw tall clocks after the latter moved from his native Somerset County in 1779. When last seen, one such clock had his label pasted on the inside of the pendulum door. A bill of sale for the clock is signed by Brokaw and dated March 22, 1780.

After a short-lived partnership with John Mann of one year from May, 1792, during which time he was a resident of Newark, Gray returned to Elizabethtown. The *New Jersey Journal,* in 1795, carried his notice as a cabinetmaker. At the same time he offered for sale "looking glasses in gilt and mahogany frames, sawmill, cross-cut and every other kind of saw, with a general assortment of Ironmongery suitable for cabinetmakers and joiners, as well as a few articles of Dr. Goods, Groceries and Crockery."

After finding time also to engage in real estate deals and several other endeavors, Gray sold his stock and business to Burrows & Howell in 1803 and was elected to the Board of Aldermen in Elizabethtown in 1808. After offering his house and lot for sale in February, 1810, he had a notice the following August in the Palladium of Liberty, in Morristown, for the sale of:

> Four cargoes of good Albany boards, Planks, Joices and Plastering Lath, and some wide, clear stuff.

He died June 21, 1818, and is buried in St. John's graveyard in Elizabethtown. An inventory and notice of sale in August of that year includes:

> 2 odd chairs, a looking glass, 2 odd tables, ½ dozen Mahogany Chairs, Mahogany Wardrobe, 1 pr. large looking glasses, clock and case valued at $20, Mahogany Desk, Side Board, 8 fancy chairs, 1 mahogany tea table, 1 candle stand, Mahogany knife box, 2 tea caddies, 3 Tea Boards, 15 old chairs, Beauroe & Bookcase, 1 old Breakfast Table, round Tea Table, Corner Cup Board, 3 old Tables, Kitchen Dressers.

The inventory provides some indication of the possessions of a hand craftsman, merchant, and businessman of modest circumstances in New Jersey in the early 1800s.

Elihu Britten was a cabinetmaker working in New Jersey between 1805 and 1820, according to newspaper files and church records of the period. Born in Elizabethtown in 1778, he married Mary Price, daughter of a stone carver, on December 14, 1799, and his second wife was Albina Ralston. The *New Jersey Journal,* in May, 1805, carried the following notice:

> Britten & Meeker intend continuing the cabinet making business in all its various branches.

The same month the following appeared:

> E. Britten begs leave to thank the public for their past favors, and requests a continuance of them to the firm of Britten & Meeker.

A month later a notice dissolving the partnership appeared along with the offer of "a reward of $25 for the apprehension of a runaway apprentice boy to the cabinet making business, by name Ludlow Pierson."

During the same period an apprentice who apparently stayed with him was Caleb Carter Burroughs. After completing an apprenticeship, Burroughs set up shop in what is now Madison. A documented chest made by him reflects an excellent knowledge of his craft, including the use of inlay and veneer.

A bill of payment dated March 18, 1819, for receipt of $20 from Mathias Burnet on account toward payment for a bureau indicates that Britten was active at least until that time. He died on November 9, 1849. An entry in the Burroughs books in 1820 shows that a half day's work on a coffin cost two shillings, or twenty-eight cents. In those days every cabinetmaker had to make coffins and even perform the role of undertaker.

Another cabinetmaker-undertaker in the area was Elias B. Sturges, who was born in 1803 and died in 1882. He lived in what is present-day Chatham, in a house at the entrance of what is now Roosevelt Avenue. Other cabinetmakers in the township early in the nineteenth century were Bregmar Gustav, a native of France; Richard T. Brown, an Englishman; Stephen B. Wilkenson; Timothy Day, who advertised in the *New Jersey Journal,* and David Miller. An inventory of the Miller estate after his death in 1815 listed unfinished bureaus, fancy chairs, and cabinet mountings.

These men had other occupations. When they were not engaged in woodworking, they were farmers, fishermen, carpenters, and even broom makers.

John Jelliff was an outstanding cabinetmaker in Newark during much of the nineteenth century. Born in Norwalk, Connecticut, he was apprenticed to a cabinetmaker in New York City and removed to New Jersey in the early 1820s. He worked first for Lemuel L. Crane, who had a woodworking shop at 333 Broad Street. He is listed in the first Newark city directory in 1835 as living with his widowed mother at 9 Court Street, where he also worked as a cabinetmaker.

Jelliff had a chance to take over the Crane business in 1838 and in the city directory for that year he is listed as in partnership with Thomas Van Tilburg. They are described as: "Manufacturers and Dealers in Furniture, Mahogany Chairs, Sofas, Mattresses, etc."

Jelliff and Van Tilburg parted company in 1843, with Jelliff staying on at the old address. Five years after he took over the David Alling business from heirs in 1855, he sold the establishment to Peter G. McDermit and it became just another of Newark's many furniture houses.

The same year, in 1860, Jelliff took as a partner Henry H. Miller, who had been his foreman. They carried on a large business, catering to the needs of the leading families in Newark and environs. He retired in 1890 and died July 2, 1893.

One of the best-known undertakings of the Jelliff & Miller partnership is a parlor suite now in the refurnished Ballentine House, which adjoins and is part of the Newark Museum. Consisting of a sofa, armchair, and four side chairs, it was made in the 1870s for the James Coe family, then living at 698 High Street. They were descendants of Benjamin Coe, who settled in Newark in 1732.

A cherry cupboard-on-chest recently acquired from a local source by the Monmouth County Historical Association is on display in its building opposite the Revolutionary battle monument in Freehold. It is a splendid example of the work of Oliver Parsell, eighteenth-century cabinetmaker in New Jersey.

Born on Long Island in 1757, Parsell learned his trade with Duncan Phyfe in New York City, where he is recorded in 1797. Later he bought a farm in Neshanic, in Hunterdon county.

From Neshanic he moved to New Brunswick, although the precise date is not known. From his shop in Church street, that city, he turned out a variety of furniture for nearly two decades. Death came on May 18, 1818, and his grave is in the Dutch Reformed churchyard in New Brunswick.

Parsell was a contemporary of Matthew Egerton, Jr., a native Jerseyan whose home was on Schurman Street in New Brunswick. They competed for the trade of families in the surrounding area of Middlesex and Monmouth counties and up the Raritan Valley into neighboring Somerset, Hunterdon, and parts of Morris counties.

Marlpit Hall

The cupboard now in the museum at Freehold is known to have been made by Parsell around 1800 and is one of the first he made after setting up shop in New Brunswick. It is cherry, a wood native to New Jersey and favored by its craftsmen. More important, it has a Parsell label; labeled furniture always claims special attention.

Pasted on the inside of an upper door, the label reads:

Oliver Parsell—Cabinet Maker—Church Street—New Brunswick.

The label definitely fixes the maker and location. The date could not have been before 1799, when Parsell was first in New Brunswick.

The cupboard has molded, paneled doors. Beneath the chest section, which includes three doors, are bracket feet that flare out sharply. The drawer handles, each emblazoned with the figure of an eagle, are believed to be original.

In a Red Bank antique shop I once came across a Winthrop-style cherry desk. It had an oval label of an "Alexander Moore, cabinetmaker, Church & Queen streets, New Brunswick." Research discloses that the city's charter, dated 1730, names him as chamberlain (treasurer) under Thomas Farmer, the city's first mayor. As yet nothing further has come to light as to where he learned his craft, dates of birth and death, or the years he worked in the Middlesex County city.

4

Clocks and Clockmakers

*A*lthough much has been written about early American
clockmakers, only scant attention has been given
to those sturdy members of the craft who were in New
Jersey during the latter part of the eighteenth and early
part of the nineteenth centuries. There were more than
two-score of them, and splendid examples of their work are
to be found.

The art of clockmaking was practically full grown when
it reached America. The first of the craft was William
Davis, who hung out his sign for business in Boston in 1683;
it was more than half a century later before others were
working in New Jersey. By that time the colonies were
about midway in the era stretching roughly from 1700 to
1800, during which time tall clocks were the generally
accepted instruments for measuring time.

There were a few of the so-called lantern and bracket
type of clocks in New Jersey, but they were all either of
New England or foreign origin. As a matter of fact, many
of the tall clocks were made outside the state, but the
craftsmen with whom we will deal met most of the demand
from about 1760 until well into the nineteenth century.

A surprisingly large proportion of the New Jersey clockmakers were silversmiths as well, and gradually they turned

their talents in that direction. After 1825 the popularity of the grandfather type began to wane, and the mantel clock, and also the banjo clock, found favor with Jerseymen. Instead of following the trend of the times, it appears that most of the native clockmakers turned more and more to the jewelry business. They kept shops that offered trinkets and a variety of other wares, including the smaller shelf and wall clocks, which were turned out in ever-increasing numbers by Eli Terry, Seth Thomas, and others in Connecticut. Here and there a veteran of the hand-made period continued to fashion tall clocks on order, but no group of younger men arose to succeed them and apprentices in the trade became for the most part purveyors and repairers of the new styles from Connecticut, where the clockmaking industry came to center.

Many of the early New Jersey clockmakers were unknown when I first undertook to find out about them, and several were credited by some authorities to other sections. Aid in identifying them came from an unexpected quarter in the person of a one-time New York business man. Tiring of the prosaic task of keeping books in a bank, he turned to repairing clocks, after the exacting manner learned in his youth as an apprentice in his father's shop.

In company and separately, the two of us covered a large part of the state in a search for old clocks. He put in running order those which needed only the touch of a familiar hand, while I concentrated on gathering information about the makers. Some we found were turned out by Eli Terry, the Willards, and contemporary New Englanders, while others were of English origin, brought to this country by colonial ancestors. More important, we located some tall, graceful grandfather clocks in their mahogany and cherry cases that had been produced by Jerseymen.

It is difficult arbitrarily to place any Jersey clockmaker in the forefront as master of his craft, because each of them has left behind excellent examples. The group includes Aaron Miller and Isaac Brokaw of Elizabethtown; Aaron

Brokaw of near-by Rahway (Bridge Town); Joachim Hill of Flemington, in Hunterdon County; William Leslie and contemporaries in Trenton; John Nicholl of Belvidere, and Peter Lupp (Leupp) of New Brunswick.

In common with other clockmakers of the times, those in New Jersey did not undertake the making of cases. They depended on experts in cabinet work, hence we find examples of such skilled craftsmen as Mathew Egerton and his son of New Brunswick and James Topping of Chester. Undoubtedly other cabinetmakers helped to meet the demand, but the frequent absence of labels and the necessity of depending only on details of construction make identification difficult.

The first definite record of a New Jersey clockmaker is the following advertisement, which appeared in the *New York Gazetteer* of November 23, 1747:

Aaron Miller, clockmaker in Elizabethtown, East Jersey, makes and sells all sorts of clocks after the Dutch manner, with expedition. He likewise makes compasses and chains for surveyors; as also bells of any size, he having a foundry for that purpose and has cast several who have been approved to be good; and will supply any person on a timely notice with any of the above articles at any reasonable rate.

Miller was of Dutch extraction and went to Elizabethtown from New York, where he learned his trade. His clocks are rare, but those attributed to him show evidence of splendid workmanship. The best example known to the writer stands about seven feet high and is finished in mahogany. Its design is simple, with few embellishments except a conservatively scrolled top adorned with three brass balls, the middle surmounted by the small figure of an eagle. The hours are indicated with Roman numerals, and the face is designed for declaring the phases of the moon and days of the month.

The account books of Samuel Woodruff, then treasurer of the First Presbyterian Church in Elizabethtown, show that in the spring of 1759, a public clock was installed by Aaron Miller in the belfry of the structure. Although no charge is recorded for his work, £10.6.9. is shown as the expense of painting the one face and for carpentry. A separate item of £1.8.9. is listed for a "clock rope."

The dates of Aaron Miller's arrival in Elizabethtown and his marriage to Elizabeth Hatfield, descendant of one of its pioneer families, are not known. Apparently he was in business for many years and is supposed to have taught his trade to a grandson, Kennedy Miller, son of Robert Miller, who did not become a clockmaker. Clocks of the younger Miller had the characteristic inlay that marked most of those made in Jersey. In addition they had under the hood an eagle and sixteen stars.

In his will, dated August 28, 1777, Aaron Miller left part of his clockmaking tools to his son-in-law, Isaac Brokaw, husband of his daughter, Elizabeth.

Brokaw was born in Raritan, Somerset County, in 1746, and died in 1826. As a young man he went to Elizabethtown and became apprenticed to Miller. Isaac Brokaw's marriage to the daughter of Aaron Miller was blessed by three sons, one named Aaron after his grandfather, Cornelius, and John. Isaac began his trade in Elizabeth around 1770 and remained there until 1790, when he removed to Bridge Town, on the south side of the Rahway River, which is now known as Rahway. The tall clocks he made in Elizabeth are marked "Isaac Brokaw, Elizabethtown" and those made in Bridge Town are marked "Isaac Brokaw, Bridge Town." His clocks rank high in quality and one of the best examples remains in the possession of the Miller family, whose members continue to live in New Jersey. It has the familiar Brokaw dial, with Roman numerals to indicate the hours. It shows also the phases of the moon and the days of the month, and the maker's name is across the bottom, followed by the word *Elizabethtown*.

The elder son, Aaron, was working as a clockmaker in Bridge Town as early as 1805 and the second son, John,

Isaac Brokaw tall clock

Aaron Lane tall clock

was in business with him in 1810. Aaron's earliest clocks
are marked "Aaron Brokaw, Bridge Town" and those of
later make "Aaron Brokaw, Rahway, E. J.," the initials
standing for East Jersey. One of John's clocks, still in good
running order, has a pewter dial.

For cases, the Brokaws went to the Egertons at New
Brunswick, Rousett & Mulford, cabinetmakers in Elizabethtown, and John Scudder, who lived on the Rahway-Westfield Road.

Another clockmaker of Elizabethtown was Aaron Lane.
He was a silversmith, and some of his clocks are to be distinguished by the silver dials he made. He worked on clocks
between 1780 and 1793, with his brother-in-law, Ichabod
Williams, furnishing the cases. On the clocks with painted
dials his name appears across the top of the face, Elizabethtown at the bottom.

The clocks of Joachim Hill must have been in high favor
during the many years he worked at Flemington, in Hunterdon County. Those bearing his name are to be found quite
frequently, almost always in good condition. He was born
November 25, 1783, on a farm in Amwell, near Flemington, the son of Isaac and Mary Hill. The manner in which
he acquired his trade, and where, are not known, but records
indicate that he first worked about 1800.

As a maker of eight-day clocks, Hill was known over the
Jersey countryside for more than fifty years. His place of
business was a brick building on Copper Hill, directly across
the street from where he lived with his wife and seven
children. It was a casting shop, with a huge bellows and
an engine he made himself for turning out parts of the brass
works for his clocks.

Hill purchased many of the cases for his clocks from
James Topping, a contemporary of the period, in Chester.
The dials he also bought, but he made the movements and
did the assembling. He undertook to repair his clocks and
observed the custom of journeying on horseback over a
large section of countryside to keep them in running order.

Joachim Hill tall clock

Local history records him as a man of very short stature, with dark eyes and heavy black hair. Late in life he removed to Newark to live with a daughter and, following his death at the age of eighty-six years in 1869, he was buried in the Presbyterian Cemetery at Flemington.

Hill's clocks are inscribed with the name and address of the maker on the lower part of the dial, directly beneath the place indicating the days of the month. In contrast to those of other makers, the dials have figures to indicate the hours and at the top they are designed for declaring phases of the moon. The cases of mahogany, with decorative inlay, have well-turned columns of good proportions along the sides, and the top finishes off with a conservative scroll adorned with three brass balls. At the top and rear of all Hill clocks there is an opening directly behind the gong to improve the tone of the strike.

Hunterdon County had three other early clockmakers, although none of them appears to have left so permanent a record as Hill.

The first of the trio was George Rea, who was born on a farm near Pittstown, Hunterdon County, in 1774. Where he learned his trade is not known, but he had a shop for many years until his death in 1838. The only clock definitely attributable to him is dated 1796. He is buried in the Baptist churchyard at Flemington.

Richard Hooley worked in Flemington for a short time as a clockmaker after his arrival with a group of English colonists in 1796. Later he went to Cambridge, Massachusetts, and died there in 1840.

During the same period Thomas Williams had a clockmaker's shop in Flemington, and it is claimed by historians of the county that his apprentice was Joachim Hill, but this has not been established definitely. His place was on what is now William Street, a thoroughfare named after him. So much is known from records of old deeds and advertisements, but concerning his birth or death nothing has been learned.

William J. Leslie is known to have worked in Trenton beginning in 1799. Prior to that time he was for a short period in New Brunswick and came originally from Philadelphia, where there was a clockmaker of the same family name.

In Trenton, Leslie first established quarters in a shop on Warren Street previously occupied by another clockmaker, named Joseph Yates. From advertisements in Trenton newspapers of the time, it would appear that Leslie remained in business until 1817. Some time after that year he opened a tavern in the same city.

Leslie was in partnership both in New Brunswick and in Trenton with a man named Williams, and newspaper advertisements stated that the clock cases were made by the Egertons. One notice in the *Trenton Federalist* included the rather humorous announcement that he was not "from London, Paris or Boston, but a native of New Jersey." The same advertisement offered places for two apprentices, with "boys from the country preferred." Between 1807 and 1810 Leslie was a town marshal and assessor. He died in Trenton, at sixty-two years of age, in 1831.

Around the turn of the nineteenth century Trenton had a number of clockmakers who advertised in the *Federalist*. Erastus Emmons, whose shop was near Leslie's establishment, had a notice in the issue of July 16, 1807, indicating that "all orders in the line of clock repairing will be thankfully received and punctually executed."

Joseph Giles gave notice on October 21, 1804, of a change in address to Market Street, and J. L. Newton, formerly of London, that he had opened a shop as a watchmaker and gilder.

Joseph Yates, to whom I have previously referred, was a partner in Yates & Kent, in Trenton, in 1789, and remained in business until 1803, when he removed to Freehold, Monmouth County. John Parry, originally of Philadelphia, worked in Trenton around 1789; others were John Probasco, said to have been the town's first clockmaker, and

James Huston, who was employed in his shop. Together they are said to have made the first clock in Trenton. It originally was placed in the steeple of the First Presbyterian Church and later at the old city hall.

Hugh Ely was another early clockmaker in Trenton. He was first in business at New Hope, Pennsylvania, in 1800 and later moved to Trenton, where he made clocks with music-box attachments. One of the earliest Trenton clockmakers was Jacob Maus, who haled from Philadelphia and advertised in the Trenton papers beginning in 1780. At the start he was located on the corner of Broad and State Streets, later in Warren Street.

One of the few early clockmakers in Newark was Benjamin Cleveland. Little of his life is known except that he is understood to have been an ancestor of Grover Cleveland, President of the United States, who was born at Caldwell, New Jersey. He was of New England ancestry, born in 1767 and died in Newark in 1837.

Smith Burnet had a clockmaking and repair shop on Broad Street, Newark, in 1794, as is shown by a map of the thoroughfare for that time. There undoubtedly were other makers and repairers of clocks in the early days of Newark, but history records G. R. & B. Dowling as the only contemporaries. They are listed between 1830 and 1832.

Few details are known concerning the life of John Nicholl, who was located at Belvidere, in the northwestern part of the state, from 1825 to 1860. He was of Scotch parentage and is thought to have learned the trade of clockmaker in New York. One of the best examples of his work was acquired originally about 1835 by a Joseph Nicholl, who lived in that city. It has come down in the family to a great-granddaughter living in New Jersey, and it is in excellent condition.

Nicholl followed the custom of putting his name and address on the lower part of the clock dials, which were ornately embellished, with moon showing in color directly

John Nicholl tall clock

over the hours of the day. There is no way of telling by whom the cases were made, because none have been found with labels, but they followed closely the style of the David Rittenhouse clocks made in Philadelphia. Usually they are of mahogany, with satinwood inlay, and turned columns at the top are surmounted by a gracefully curved pediment and a center finial.

In the southern part of the state one of the first clockmakers was Isaac Pearson. He was in Burlington around 1740 and in that year his daughter, Sarah, married Joseph Hollinshead, another member of the trade. The two men formed a partnership and the clocks they made were marked Pearson & Hollinshead. The Hollinshead clocks are distinguished by his name engraved on a raised circular plate fastened to the top of the dial. One of them known to the writer bears the repair mark of Joachim Hill and the year 1845 on the inside of the case.

Pearson was a gold and silversmith also, and he apparently gave little time to clocks, because only four have been found with his name. Those made by Hollinshead, some of which show his address as Moorestown, are more numerous. In general they followed the design of early New England clocks and had walnut, cherry, or mahogany cases.

Joseph Hollinshead was the earliest of at least nine clockmakers by the same name, all related, who made clocks in South Jersey. The progenitors of the family in that region were John and Grace Hollinshead, who left Connecticut in the 1680s to settle on the Rancocas Creek. Joseph, a younger son, appears to have brought up five boys in the trade, and three members of the next generation followed in his footsteps.

John Hollinshead, eldest son of Joseph, was born about 1745, Jacob in 1747, Joseph, Jr., in 1751, Hugh in 1753, and Morgan in 1757. The first spent most of his life in Burlington. Jacob married in 1772 and moved to Salem, where he opened a shop. Joseph, Jr., stayed in Burlington, while Hugh started to make clocks in Mount Holly and

Joseph Hollinshead tall clock

later went to Moorestown, where Morgan had located. The two younger brothers both married in 1775, and Morgan is known to have died in 1832.

Morgan Hollinshead numbered his clocks on the dial and about twenty of them are known to be in existence. He had a son, George, who followed the same custom after marrying in 1820 and setting up a shop in Woodstown. Job was another son, and he is known to have learned the trade, although none of his clocks have been found for a certainty. Clocks made by all the other Hollinsheads and a few bearing the partnership name of Pearson & Hollinshead are scattered through South Jersey, and occasionally may be seen across the Delaware River in Pennsylvania.

The pioneer clockmaker of Bordentown was Samuel Shourds, who was in the town beginning sometime in the 1740s. The only clock thus far located with his name is in the home of a Moorestown family.

In addition to the Hollinsheads, Mount Holly was the home of David Shoemaker, who made clocks during the 1760s. Another clockmaker was Joshua Budd, who moved his shop from New Mills (now Pemberton) after the Revolution.

Other Mount Holly clockmakers have been identified as Richard Dickenson, Daniel Fling, and Peter Hill. Clocks bearing the names of these three men are known to exist, but comparatively little is known concerning the makers. In Dr. Zachariah Reed's *Annuals,* written in 1859, reference is made to Hill and it is stated that his shop was located on the west side of Main Street, near Mill Street. Records of the Quaker burying ground in Burlington mention a Peter Hill, who was a Negro and the only one of his race in those days who learned the trade of a watch and clockmaker. It appears likely, however, that there were two Peter Hills, because the first mentioned was for a time in Mount Holly and a white man.

Benjamin Reeve was a clockmaker in Greenwich between 1750 and 1790, and a number of clocks of excellent workmanship, with mahogany or cherry cases and his name on the dial, have been found in different parts of South Jersey. There is one of his in the Wood's Mansion in Greenwich and another in the home of a descendant living in Moorestown.

There were two clockmakers by the name of Hudson who worked in Mount Holly during the last quarter of the eighteenth century. One was William and the other Edward. They were brothers, who had learned their trade in Philadelphia from a John Wood. The clocks made by the Hudsons were unusually tall, with cases of mahogany or walnut, and they were marked with the address in addition to the name.

Early Burlington records refer to the will of John Willis, clockmaker of that town, filed in 1748, but no examples of his work are known to exist.

Two makers of tall clocks are recorded in the early history of Woodbury, in Gloucester County. A John Whitehead was located there in the 1750s, and Isaac Cooper was there around 1770. Examples of their work are rare.

Hurtin & Burgi are listed in the early records of Bound Brook, Somerset County. They had a shop in the village as early as 1766. According to tradition they kept in repair the timepieces of Washington and the officers of his army during the winter of 1778, when they were in winter quarters in the vicinity.

One of the few clockmakers of Monmouth County in colonial times was Elias Sayre, who had a shop in Middletown in the 1780s. His time recorders are popularly called Monmouth clocks, because he showed that single word on the dials to indicate his address. The tall cases were well made of cherry or mahogany, but in the absence of labels, it is impossible to say by whom they were made. One of the clocks, with a sailing vessel adorning the dial, is in the Monmouth County Historical Society building at Freehold.

Several tall case clocks in excellent condition have been found bearing the name of Uriah Gould, who had a shop in

Elias Sayre tall clock

Peter Lupp tall clock

Mendham, Morris County, during the first years of the nineteenth century.

Records of Rahway in 1827 list John Pressaq as a maker and repairer of clocks in that town.

New Brunswick may claim three on the list of early New Jersey clockmakers. They were all members of the Leupp family. The first was Louis, who immigrated from Germany prior to the Revolution and opened a shop in Albany Street. He was a silversmith as well, and three sons, Henry, Samuel, and Peter, followed in his footsteps. They will be discussed more fully in the chapter devoted to silversmiths.

The *New Brunswick Advertiser* of March 27, 1798, lists Charles Wheeler and Isaac Reed as clock and watchmakers.

Michael Hacker was a Moravian who settled in New Germantown (Oldwick), Hunterdon County, in the 1750s. Some of his tall clocks have been found dated as early as 1757, with either "New Germantown" or "Tewksbury" for address. He died in 1796.

Mathias Baldwin, born at Elizabethtown on December 10, 1795, spent his entire career as a clockmaker and inventor in Philadelphia. Apprenticed at the age of sixteen years, he was operating his own shop by nineteen and in 1831 made a model steam locomotive that led to the founding of the Baldwin Locomotive Works.

George Washington Coppuck, a maker of tall clocks, was working about 1825 at Mount Holly, and Samuel Baker had a shop at several locations in New Brunswick from 1822 to 1858.

A clockmaker of the 1840-50s, native to New Jersey, was Aaron Dodd Crane, descendant of a pioneer Newark family. Born in Caldwell on May 8, 1804, he was the youngest of seven children. While still living in Caldwell, his first patent was issued. Presumably lost when the Patent Office in Washington was burned in 1836, it was for a pendulum clock. The next recorded event in his life was his marriage to Sarah Campbell in the Caldwell Presbyterian

Church on January 12, 1831.

Crane was listed as a clockmaker in directories for 1842-43 and again in 1843-44. In 1845 a *History of Essex and Hudson Counties* credits him with inventing a one-year clock, which was produced by James F. Mills & Co. Directories in Newark from 1849-57 show that he lived at 6 Lombardy Street in that city. In 1857-58 he was a clockmaker in Boston.

Ezra Woodruff, a clockmaker in Elizabethtown between 1808-17, was born on January 14, 1787, the son of Enos and Charity (Ogden) Woodruff, according to family Bible records. His trade was learned from his father, who was a partner of William Dawes. A notice in the *New Jersey Journal* in 1804 reads:

> The firm of Dawes & Woodruff carry on the different branches of Clock and Watch making.

Ezra Woodruff followed other crafts. An inventory of the estate of John Burnet of Elizabethtown in 1813 lists him as recipient of "a set of coachmaker's tools, wheels and hub benches." He moved to Cincinnati, Ohio, shortly before 1820 and later to Louisville, Kentucky, where he operated a brass foundry and may well have turned out clockworks of that metal.

I know of a single tall clock bearing the name "Ezra Woodruff" on the dial. Inlay and decorations on the case date it from about 1810.

Samuel Gamage, who was working in Elizabethtown from 1805 until 1814, was a native of Cambridge, Massachusetts, where he was born April 16, 1782. He advertised first in the *New Jersey Journal* in May, 1805, as a clock and watchmaker, gold and silversmith, as follows:

> Samuel Gamage begs leave to inform the public, that he has lately taken a shop adjoining the Store of Burrows & Howell, two doors from the Post Office, where he intends carrying on the above business in its various branches, and hopes by his strict attention to receive a liberal patronage. All those who please to

favor him with their custom may depend on being served with punctuality and dispatch.

After offering cash for gold and silver, the notice lists the following articles for sale:

Warranted clocks and watches, watch chains, seals, keys, trinkets, Silver and Plated Tea and Table Spoons, Silver and Plated Sugar Tongs, plated Knives and Forks, gold and gilt ear knobs and Hoops of various descriptions, finger rings, breast pins, silver Thimbles, brass ladies' elegant Medallions, lockets, Morocco Thread Cases and purses of various kinds, horn and tortoise shell combs, pearls, garnets, cut glass and Spain Beads, gold and silver Spangles, violin strings, snuff, tobacco and segar boxes, silver Fruit Knives, counting house plated Knives, polished steel and silver pencil cases, lead pencils and numerous other articles.

As though that was not enough to show what was offered by a well-stocked handcraft shop in the early 1800s, Gamage advertised again in 1806 that he continued in business at the old stand. After listing again the articles for sale and adding such items as toothbrushes, scissors, and toothpicks, he concluded with an appeal for "Two or more Journeymen."

Announcement of his marriage to Julia Tunis on May 22, 1808, appeared several days later. The next record lists him at 115 Liberty Street, New York City; in 1819 he removed to Batavia County, Ohio, where he died in 1824. Examples of his work are not known to me.

William P. Dawes was a clockmaker as well as a part-time gold and silversmith. He married Sarah Miller, granddaughter of Aaron Miller, best-known Jersey clockmaker of colonial times, in April, 1811. Records indicate that Dawes was quite a competent craftsman in his own right. A native of England, he came to America during the Revolution and notices in the *New Jersey Journal* indicate that he worked in Elizabethtown between 1803 and 1814.

The first notice appeared on February 10, 1803, and read:

To let—The House and Shop, near the stone bridge, in Elizabethtown, where Mr. William Dawes now lives, from the first day of April next.

A year later the following notice appeared:

The subscribers take this method of informing the Public that they have entered into a line of their profession under the firm name of Dawes & Woodruff, in Elizabethtown, at the shop formerly occupied by Robinson Thomas as a store, where they carry on the different branches of Watch and Clock Making and Silver-Plating on the most accommodating terms; and they flatter themselves by a steady attention to business, they will receive a proportionate share of the liberality of the Public.

N.B. Any quantity or quality of articles in the above business may be had at their shop on the shortest notice.

Notice of the partnership's end was given in April, 1805, and nine years later, in April, 1814, the following notice appeared:

House and Lot—The late property of William Dawes are offered for sale.

There is nothing to indicate whether Dawes, the craftsman, or a son who bore his name moved to Ackquackoon Township, but in January, 1830, it was announced that he and his wife had sold to Cornelius Miller Dawes for $500 a lot on the Hamburg-Paterson Turnpike "next to the graveyard."

The following October Cornelius Miller Dawes and his wife, Phoebe, of Orange, sold to a Cornelius whose last name is illegible, for $30 "A lot in Acq. on Hamburg-Paterson Tpke. whereon William P. Dawes now lives next the graveyard."

A finely made tall clock, with iron dial bearing the name of William Dawes, was offered for sale in a New York City gallery several years ago and the present owner is not known. Its inlaid Hepplewhite-style case had no label, although it resembled Jersey-made cases of the Federal era.

A shop on South 17th Street, Philadelphia, listed a few months ago "a supurb mahogany tall clock." Across the dial it had "William Crow, Salem, N.J." Nothing is known about him aside from the fact that a memorandum acquired by the dealer along with the clock declared it to be the only known example of his work, dating from 1735 to 1740.

5

Chairs and Chairmakers

*C*hairmaking was an art followed in various parts of
New Jersey beginning with the earliest settlements.
There is no telling just when, where, or by whom the first
such articles of furniture were turned out, because they were
made as necessity required, when the demand could not be
filled quickly enough from abroad and before skilled workers had come in to set up in business.

Made by the men of the family possessing the most ability and as they were able to take time out from other tasks,
the earliest of the native chairs followed the English and
Dutch styles. The first settlers in northern Jersey were of
those two nationalities and it was to be expected that they
would seek to reproduce the things to which they had been
accustomed. As a matter of fact, succeeding generations
copied the chairs to which they fell heir and it was well
into the nineteenth century before independence in design
was displayed.

Although chairs had been known to the world long before,
by introduction from Constantinople, and had passed
through various stages of evolution, they were just coming
into general use when New Jersey began to attract colonists
in the last quarter of the seventeenth century. It was thought
to be good for people to sit erect on joined stools, and chairs

Hudson County elder's chair

were reserved for special occasions. The oldest that are known to have survived from those days were the so-called "elder" chairs. A few of them are preserved by the churches where they were first used, and several are in the hands of descendants of the God-fearing men who once sat in them at each Sunday service.

The rod, banister, and slat-back chairs, probably developed from the Pilgrim and Brewster chairs of New England, were favored for many years in New Jersey. They were made also in other sections of the colonies over a period of considerably more than one hundred years, and the lack of identifying marks leaves only family tradition or history as a means of making their origin certain.

From the Dutch influence out of Niew Amsterdam, the slat-back, rush-bottomed chair, with plainly turned backposts and cross rungs and without arms, was from the first common in that region bordering along the Hudson and again in the central portion of the state. As the years went on, certain families in the more important towns prospered, and they turned to more comfortable styles, but the inhabitants of rural areas contained to make daily use of the plainer chairs up to and even after the Civil War.

As a rule the slat-back chairs were made with four crosspieces at the back, although occasionally five or three were used. Those of simpler construction had plainly turned uprights and rungs, and only the chairs for the heads of the family were given the added distinction and comfort of arms. Ash, oak, and hickory were most frequently used.

The slat-back chair was made extensively in Monmouth County for many years and numerous examples have been attributed definitely to various craftsmen. Fashioned from ash and other local hard woods, they have withstood wear and time in a manner to do credit to the sturdiness of construction. For the most part they were made with the familiar rush-bottom seat, but occasionally one may be found with leather.

Clayton's shop at Allentown turned out many of the slat-

Three types of New Jersey rush-bottom chair

back chairs for Monmouth County folk of 1780-1800. At Englishtown there were Pierson Thompson, John Leonard, and J. Davidson Herbert.

The banister-back was another type of chair made in New Jersey. Coming by way of New England near the end of the William and Mary period, it found considerable favor in the southern part of the state. It was more elaborate than the slat-back, although it retained the rush-bottomed seat. The rear uprights, squared at the bottom, extended further and were surmounted usually by a carved cross-piece, which often was in the form of a sunburst. At the back were four or five vertical half-spindles, with the flat side toward the front. Such chairs were made both with and without arms. The turnings were of the ball and vase design.

Mostly hard woods were used for the banister-backs, which were the vogue from 1700 for nearly half a century. They were finished by a variety of methods, although painting in black and sometimes other colors was most in favor.

Next came the fiddle-back and cabriole chair of the Queen Anne period. It got its name from a single back splat shaped much like a violin, although in reality it was of a vase design on account of the bulge of the front legs. Various adaptations included rush or cloth seats, straight legs, and turned or smooth uprights in front and rear. Those of more elaborate make in mahogany were favored in the towns along the coast, and the plainer designs in native woods sufficed in the interior.

About the time that the Queen Anne period was nearing a close, chairs began to have more style. The front legs were ornamented with carving and armchairs were made with cabinet woods varnished and polished at the exposed parts. The Chippendale era saw further changes, and styles were so altered to suit the whims of makers and purchasers that it is difficult to identify either the locality where they were made or the craftsmen.

As the years progressed the aim of chairmakers was comfort. Upholstered seats came to be the general rule except in the plainer pieces, and most of those with arms had covered backs. Chairs were made in several sizes for the men and womenfolk and the latter had such innovations as flaring sides to make room for the ladies' skirts. Leather was used for upholstery material, and also various kinds of damask, tapestry, and even haircloth.

Occasionally chairs are found with the makers' labels, but they have been very few. For the most part, identification of a particular chair with its maker depends upon family history or tradition.

The Revolution came on while the so-called Chippendale style was favored for the better-made chairs. For the next decade it is doubtful if much attention was given to new pieces and most certainly in New Jersey, where fighting was most frequent, the work was limited to those of plainer design. It is hardly likely that many of these survived the years.

After the war was over there was a revival of the market for chairs and they began to exhibit more skill in construction. The Hepplewhite style came in to add grace, with fine curves for the back, straight lines in the body, and tapered legs. Reeding, carving, and inlay came to be used. Mahogany was a favorite wood along the coast, and cherry in the rural sections.

The Hepplewhite style merged at the turn of the nineteenth century into the Sheraton and was followed by the French Directoire. Duncan Phyfe and other leading American cabinetmakers adapted the lines to chairs, with the lyre, palm, shield, and other designs by way of variation. They set other makers to following their own ideas and the result was a general breaking away from distinctive style.

Early in the 1800s the first typical American development in chairmaking came with fancy painting. Hitchcock started the vogue in New England and soon such chairs were being turned out in large quantities. They remained in favor when the American Empire style came along and at about the same time the rocking chair became a desired piece of furniture in every household.

Chairmaking was an important industry in Newark after the nineteenth century came in and, according to records of a census in 1826, there were seventy-nine such craftsmen by that time. Most of them worked at the factory of David Alling, who had a reputation for style and workmanship. He specialized in the painted chair and not only supplied a large home trade, but catered to an extensive demand in the South.

Throughout New Jersey and particularly in the central counties are to be found chairs of undoubted local make, but as to the craftsmen who fashioned them there is no way of determining. They are for the most part of one or another of the styles or types described in preceding pages,

Boston rocker

but here and there may be found a chair that has been preserved through the generations for the patriarch of the family. Usually it is a rocker of the Windsor type, with seat of wood, curved arms, and high back. Dating from the early 1820s, it is just the sort of chair in which elderly folks might rock away their declining years in comfort.

Occasionally there may be found the double love seat. Those of plainer design, with splatted back and rush seat, were used at one time in the rear of the family wagon to carry its members to church. The painted settees of the 1830 period have mostly disappeared, but now and then one is to be found gracing the front porch of some farmhouse, after the fashion of those days when they were used to seat four or five persons of a summer evening after the day's work was finished.

A caned rocker

The Windsor chair enjoyed a special popularity over many of the years already covered. It first came to America about 1700 from England and found favor in all of the colonies. Those made in different sections had their particular characteristics and thus those from New England were very different in style from those of Pennsylvania. In New Jersey those native to the northern counties were influenced from Connecticut, while elsewhere they followed the proportions of Pennsylvania chairs.

Files of the *Guardian* or *New Brunswick Advertiser* give a clue to some of the early chairmakers in that city. The issue of May 6, 1793, listed John Ryckman, "Cabinet and Chairmaker at the upper end of Albany Street, who respectfully informs the public that he has lately removed from New York."

In the issue of June 10, 1802, Campbell Dunham offered his services as a Windsor chairmaker.

Alexander Chambers was a wood turner and chairmaker in Trenton and one of its foremost citizens from around 1763 until after the Revolution. The fact that he was a man of affairs in those days is indicated by Hunterdon court records for 1767, which list him as one of the arbitrators in a suit involving the ownership of an ironworks known as the Squires Point Forge. Chambers advertised Windsor chairs for sale, as well as those after the Hepplewhite style.

Mention should be made here of Benjamin Randolph, who has been referred to in a previous chapter as a maker of fine furniture. He is probably even better known for the excellence of his chairs and for the prices some of them have brought.

The earliest Windsors of New Jersey make were of low-back design, with a heavy rounded top rail in which ended the ten or twelve spindles fastened into the wooden seat. The legs were turned and set at an angle, with turned side pieces and stringer about three inches from the bottom to lend strength. Later, the back spindles were made higher for added comfort, and on some the right arm was widened to provide a writing surface. To strengthen the back a single spindle was run from the top rail to the seat as a brace.

The popular demand for Windsor chairs prompted some makers to cater exclusively to that trade. In 1808 the *State Gazette,* published in Trenton, carried the advertisement of William Kerwood announcing that he had a complete stock of Windsor chairs made by Samuel Moon in nearby Morrisville. In nearly every other village of any size there was a Windsor maker.

Contrary to general belief, Windsors were not made of one wood. Different varieties were used for special purposes and unseasoned wood was favored because of shrinking, which would make tighter joints. Bottoms were cut from seasoned planks of pine or whitewood, while oak, hickory, and ash were utilized for spindles, hoops, and back rails.

Following the example of craftsmen in other sections, some of the New Jersey men made Windsors with rockers, and even the settees followed that style. Then, too, there were adaptations of the Windsor style to stools and tables.

Omar Boden was a native Jerseyman who learned his trade in the state and then moved elsewhere. He was born and grew up in Burlington, where he worked until 1792. Then twenty years of age, he married Sarah Bloomfield. They moved to Cooperstown, New York, in 1799, and he operated a factory where he made fancy chairs after the Sheraton manner until 1826.

A Windsor-style bench, painted with the old buttermilk red paint, is one of the known Boden pieces. It was presented to the New York State Historical Association museum at Cooperstown in 1947 by his granddaughter, Mrs. Frederick C. Parshall, of Plattsburg, New York. Boden died in 1844 at seventy-eight years, and his wife's death came in 1858.

John Woodruff was one of the earliest woodworkers and chairmakers in New Jersey. A deed of 1715 refers to him

A Windsor rocker

as a joiner, and the flyleaf of a book of 1735 lists the owner as "Cooper Woodruff, grandson of John, the joiner."

The above-mentioned Cooper Woodruff was born in 1759 and died June 26, 1825, according to notices in the *New*

Jersey Journal and *Sentinal of Freedom*. He is buried in the First Presbyterian churchyard in Elizabeth. A wood turner and chairmaker in the Elizabethtown-Newark area until his death, he was baptized June 16, 1766, according to records of St. John's Episcopal Church in Elizabeth. The only notice found thus far referring to his trade appeared in the *New Jersey Journal* in December, 1799, and read:

> Wanted—An apprentice to the Spinning Wheel and Turning business. A lad about 14 or 15 years old; also, a Journeyman that understands Sitting Chair Making.

He was mentioned later in wills, appraisings of estates, and sales of land.

Jersey-made chairs sought by today's collectors fall into three groups—those for sitting, those for riding, and the fancy chairs. This is to say nothing of the chairs made elsewhere and sold within the state in shops and even off the tailboard of peddler wagons.

There was a time when craftsmen made a specialty of the type of chair in which they were most proficient, as witness the above-quoted notice of Cooper Woodruff. Patrons had to prescribe whether they desired chairs for sitting or riding, or whether they should be fancy or plain. Notices asking for apprentices and journeymen invariably specified the branch of work, in each instance requiring certain talents.

David Whitehead was another Elizabethtown chairmaker who went in for the different types of chairs. He advertised in March, 1801, for an apprentice to the "sitting chair business" and also a journeyman. Later on he advertised for "2 journeymen for the Fancy Chair Making Business."

Apparently Whitehead was successful in his second quest and in November, 1818, informed his friends that "in addition to his former business, he has commenced Fancy and Ornamental Chairs on hand and intends keeping an assortment of the most modern and fashionable styles." Whitehead boasted that he "employed an experienced Fancy and Ornamental Chair Maker and repairs, paints and ornaments all types of chairs."

Riding chairs were first designed to be held several feet off the ground between two rods, or poles, carried fore and aft by servants or other persons. They were enclosed, except at the front, and filled a major need from the latter part of the seventeenth century into the next when travelers moved overland along narrow trails. So far as I know, none of that particular type of riding chair exists today.

The riding chairs of the later 1700s well into the next century were known also as wagon seats. Usually of double width and with legs shorter than those of a conventional chair, they were commonly placed in wagons to hold additional persons—family members or visitors on trips to church or country fair, or to the nearest village on shopping trips. Occasionally upholstered for added comfort over dirt roads, they were more often plainly made, with rush seats and two splats across the back.

Wagon chairs are still found in rural areas. I saw one recently, apparently left behind after church services in upper Sussex County several years ago. It was found later in the church shed by a lady who now keeps it on her sun porch.

A friend who enjoyed several days last summer looking for some of the "lost towns" of South Jersey tells me he came across a wagon chair without any legs. Apparently it was held off the wagon bottom by fitting between wood blocks made fast to either side of the vehicle.

The best-known of New Jersey chairs, many of which continue in everyday use after a century or more, come within the "plain" category. Usually made of ash or other native wood, they have no arms. The back has two or more slats between upright posts that start from the floor. The seat is made of rush. I have seen them, minus seat and with a broken splat or two, returned to service with a minimum of effort, which included removal of up to six layers of paint.

Henryk Glaever was working as a chairmaker in the Crosswick Creek area of what was then Burlington County

Two chairs of New Jersey origin

as early as 1690. Apparently a native of Niew Amsterdam, he moved to Crosswick by way of Philadelphia. A turned side chair, one of a pair, marked HG on a rear leg and dated between 1690 and 1710, were included in a special exhibition of New Jersey furniture at the State Museum in Trenton during the summer of 1970.

Another noteworthy chair is in the Newark Museum. It is made in the Windsor style and the maker was Isaac Mitchell, who is known to have worked in New York City and Elizabethtown between 1789 and 1810. The chair is stamped with the initials "IM" on the under part of the seat. Until now, Mitchell has not been listed as a Jersey craftsman and he is not mentioned in any published works on chairmakers.

6

Silversmiths, Pewterers, and Jewelers

*I*t seems to be the natural course to consider New Jersey silversmiths, pewterers, and jewelers under the same heading because their work was so closely related. As a matter of fact, it appears likely that silversmiths were the nearest approach in this state to pewter makers. Certain it is that in time they came to be jewelry manufacturers to meet popular demand.

It was not until more than half a century after the first settlement that silversmiths came from other sections of the colonies and abroad. As in many other respects, the earlier inhabitants depended on members of the craft in New York and Philadelphia, or sent to England, for the few additions they could afford to family pieces.

Among the first Jersey silversmiths were John Bingham, who arrived in Salem in 1664; the Philip Syngs, father and son, residents of Cape May after 1723, and Elias Boudinot III, a resident of Princeton from 1752 to 1761 and, thereafter, until his death in 1770, with his son in Elizabethtown, where he is buried.

Others established themselves from then on in the larger towns. Successive generations of the Colemans worked in Burlington from 1776 until considerably after 1800, and at New Brunswick there were Louis Lupp and his three sons over the same period of years. Examples of silverware executed by those mentioned and by at least a dozen who were contemporary are rarities today, but pieces in museums are found occasionally and family heirlooms speak well for the quality of their work.

Pewterers are the least known of New Jersey's early craftsmen. If there were any who devoted themselves to working entirely as such, proof of it has not yet been brought to light. Undoubtedly there were some who plied the trade when pewter was in common use, because pieces of plain design and apparently local origin have been found. Just as silversmiths took to making clocks when they could, it is entirely probable that they fashioned pewterware, or repaired worn pieces.

In jewelry manufacture New Jersey was a pioneer center. The early craftsmen in that line qualified as such and learned their trade as silver and goldsmiths. They took advantage of the growing demand for articles of adornment as living conditions improved. When Epaphras Hinsdale opened a small shop in Newark around 1800, it marked the beginning of an extensive industry that continues in that city to this day.

Tracing the state's early silversmiths is not the comparatively easy task that it is in England. There were no guildhalls, where marks of the various craftsmen were recorded, and no standards of fineness that had to be maintained. Then, too, we encounter the difficulty of identifying the work of Jerseymen who sometimes failed to use any mark whatever.

Articles of silver made by the early Jersey silversmiths may be grouped as either domestic or religious. Under the first heading comes tableware, silver for drinking purposes, containers, and miscellaneous articles for personal or household use. Church silver used in the communion and other devotional services comprises the second group.

It cannot be said that members of the craft during the state's colonial era attempted to fashion the whole range of silver articles turned out by those in Boston, New York, or Philadelphia, but they did very well in what they undertook. With few exceptions there was little attempt to execute anything but the plainer pieces until after the Revolution. Then there was an effort to break away from the usual designs.

Jersey silversmiths made spoons more than anything else, judging from the number of examples to be found today. Prior to about 1770 they were in three sizes. The teaspoon was as small as the after-dinner coffee spoon, the porringer spoon was a bit smaller than the present-day dessert spoon, and the tablespoon was fashioned with a handle somewhat smaller than that of those now in use.

By 1780 spoon handles became pointed and were often

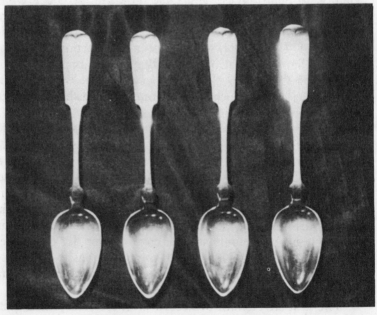

Early nineteenth-century tablespoons

engraved with bright cut decoration and initials of the owner at the top. The turn of the nineteenth century saw the coffin-handle as a popular style. After this came the fiddle-shaped handle, with a shoulder just above the junction with the bowl..

The early silversmiths were for the most part of English extraction and they followed the styles of that country, although the Dutch and to a limited degree the French influences were felt. In the sections adjacent to and more or less dependent on New York, the trend was to solid, plain pieces after the Dutch manner. Only occasionally was the highly ornate work of the few Huguenot craftsmen in favor. Over most of the state the English designs were copied.

In church silver the Dutch parts of North Jersey leaned toward use of the beaker, and there was a scarcity of the chalice. In South, West, and East Jersey, where the Church of England was strongest, the reverse was true and chalices were the rule. Occasionally there may be found an old beaker of Dutch workmanship in those sections, like the ones at St. Mary's Church in Burlington and even in a Reformed Church of the north country, but with rare exception the distinction held true. In the Swedish parishes of West Jersey the chalice was used.

Other articles of church silver showed a difference in design according to section and whether they were used by the Dutch or English, but they were for the same general purpose. There were discs or plates, either with or without rims and flat-bottomed. Usually they were in pairs and were plain patterned, except for an engraved inscription of the coat-of-arms of the donor. Flagons were tall and narrow and of tankard shape, with the cover either flat or finished in a finial. Other religious pieces were alms basins, collection plates, and baptismal bowls. There was no standard type and they varied according to the maker.

The first silversmith of record in West Jersey, and quite possibly in the entire state as we know it, was John Bingham.

He was born in England, and migrated to this country in
1664. He arrived first at Salem in Burlington County and
then removed to Evesham. Salem Deed No. 1 shows a grant
from John Fenwick to Bingham of one thousand acres April
23, 1664. Salem County records show that he married twice
and had three children. He is listed as both silversmith and
goldsmith, but no examples of his work are known.

Philip Syng, Sr., arrived in America in 1714 with his wife
and three sons. He settled at first in Philadelphia and advertised in the *American Weekly Mercury* of May 12 and
19, 1720, as a goldsmith, with a shop in Market Street.

Syng, Sr., went to Cape May in 1723 and his name is
first mentioned in the public record in connection with the
estate of Yelverton Crowell, whose inventory was dated at
Cape May on January 10, 1724. Syng, Sr., was married on
May 24, 1724, to his second wife, Hannah Leaming, of
Cape May. She died there in 1728 and soon afterward he
removed to Annapolis, Maryland, where he married a third
wife, Susannah Price, on February 26, 1733. He died at
Annapolis, May 18, 1739.

Syng, Sr., brought his first wife and three sons when he
arrived at Philadelphia and they moved with him to Cape
May. He taught all of his sons the art of silversmithing.
Philip Jr. became the greatest and best-known craftsman of
the family. He made numerous pieces of silver bearing the
letters P S in a rectangle, followed by a leaf, in a small
shield twice, with a leaf between; in a rectangle separated
by two leaves, in a combined double circle, and in script.
Some pieces have his full name in script between two leaves.

Silver pieces made by the Syngs have been found most
often among the old Quaker families in Burlington County
and in Lancaster County, Pennsylvania. A set of six tablespoons was made for Samuel and Hannah Abbott, who
were married in 1733 and lived in Elsinboro, Salem County.
Mrs. Abbott was a member of the Foster family from Burlington County and an uncle was Joseph Borden, one of the
founders of Bordentown.

Other known pieces include a silver tankard made for Joseph Saunders and Hannah (Reeves) Saunders, and tankards for Thomas and Michael Newbold, brothers who were married in Burlington County in 1724 and 1730, respectively.

Elias Boudinot, father of the Revolutionary patriot who was fourth in the family line to bear the name, was born in New York July 8, 1706, a son of Elias Boudinot and Marie Catherine Carre. His father died when he was thirteen years of age and two years later, on June 21, 1721, he was apprenticed for the customary seven-year term to Simeon Soumaine, a prominent silversmith of the day. The original indenture, dated June 6, 1722, nearly a year later, is in possession of the New York Historical Society.

After completing his apprenticeship Boudinot went to Antigua, where numerous relatives were living and from whence his grandfather, a French Huguenot, came to the United States. He was married first in Antigua on August 8, 1729, to Susannah LeRoux, who died in 1733. His second wife was Catherine Williams, who bore him six children, the third of whom was Elias Boudinot IV, president of the first Continental Congress and a most talented man.

It was shortly before 1740 that Elias Boudinot III, removed from Antigua to Philadelphia, where his son Elias IV and later children were born. On September 27, 1747, he advertised in the *Pennsylvania Gazette:*

> Elias Boudinot, Silversmith, removed from the house next to the Post Office in Market Street to the house where Mr. Joseph Noble lately dwelt in Second Street, four doors above Black Horse Alley.

Boudinot's residence in Philadelphia was near that of Benjamin Franklin and others who were destined to play a prominent part in the colonies. His interest in New Jersey early manifested itself; in 1748 it is recorded that he leased land outside New Brunswick from a Philip French, who had found virgin ore near enough to the surface that plowing turned it up. In 1751 a company he formed financed the sinking of a shaft, and for a time shipments of copper ore were sent to England. After a few years the supply was exhausted and the visions of prosperity held by those interested vanished.

In 1752-53 Elias Boudinot became a permanent resident of New Jersey by removing from Philadelphia to Princeton, where he became a leading citizen. He was postmaster of the town in 1757 and about that time came to take an interest in affairs at Elizabethtown, where Elias IV was living and practising law. On November 5, 1761, a few months prior to taking up his abode in Elizabethtown, the following advertisement appeared in the *Pennsylvania Gazette:*

> The Fourteenth part of the Copper Mine and works of New Brunswick, commonly called French's Mine, the share being clear of all charges, costs and incumbrances whatever, also, a house and lot in Princeton, a pleasant and agreeable situation, opposite the College, being 46 foot front and 36 deep with 10 rooms, 8 with fireplaces, a large new stable 40 foot long and 20 foot wide with a good well and large garden with a variety of fruit trees, a large bed of asparagus, etc., all enclosed with a good board fence, fit for a merchant or tavern. Whoever inclines to purchase may apply to Elias Boudinot of Princeton or Elias Boudinot, attorney-at-law, at Elizabethtown.

During most of the years spent at Elizabethtown, Elias Boudinot III was in failing health. In a letter written September 16, 1769, by his son to Ezekial Goldthwaite and now in possession of the Pennsylvania Historical Society, it was stated: "My father has been for many years afflicted with the dead palsy." He died on July 4, 1770, and was buried in the First Presbyterian Church graveyard in Elizabethtown beside his wife, who had passed away five years before.

It is no wonder that silver pieces executed by Elias Boudinot III are rare when his active life is considered. Those known to exist amply demonstrate how well he learned his craft. Among them is a tankard made for Benjamin

Franklin, who willed it to Dr. William Hughes. It bears the initials of Benjamin and Deborah Franklin and is on permanent loan exhibition at Franklin Institute in Philadelphia. While a resident of Princeton, about 1760, he is credited with making the Dunkin sugar bowl and Wallace tray.

The last work attributed to Elias Boudinot is a silver mug thought to have been made after 1764 for his granddaughter, Susanne, who was born in that year. She became the wife of William Bradford, attorney-general under Washington. First record of the mug appears in a cash book kept by Elias Boudinot IV. In an entry dated August 17, 1764, he wrote:

> To cash paid my father for making a silver mug, £3 light £ 2 11s. 6p.

Stephen Reeves, another one of the first silversmiths in the state, plied his trade in Burlington, when it was the provincial capital of the colony and of importance as a seaport, because all vessels for West Jersey had to enter and clear there. Silverware executed by him was in demand from 1767 until after the Revolution by prominent families of the times and was distinguished by the mark "S Reeves" in script instead of the customary block printing.

Members of the Coleman family were prominent as silversmiths in Burlington in the colonial era. The first was Nathaniel, who learned his trade in New England. He moved to Burlington from Bloomingrove, New York, prior to 1776. His brother, Benjamin, came after him around 1785, and by 1805 a son, Samuel, had learned the trade and joined with his father. All three men observed the general custom of using, as their mark, the family name prefixed by the initial of their first names. Nathaniel Coleman also marked some of his pieces with both his initials in a circle.

J. P. Fireung was a silversmith in Burlington during the

final years of the eighteenth century and on into the next until his death in 1810. Besides his mark "J. P. Fireung," he adopted the practice of a few others of his craft and followed it with the name of the town. Examples of his work are rare.

Another South Jersey silversmith, only slightly later than Reeves, was Stephen Richards. From advertisements in the *Pennsylvania Journal,* printed at Philadelphia, we learn that he was located at Cohansay Bridge, which long ago came by the name of Bridgeton. It is known that he held for sale "a fine stock of silver bowls, tankards, etc. of excellent quality." His mark "S. Richards" was used in a fringed and sometimes a straight-edged block.

The Lupps were making silver of high quality in New Brunswick during the same period as the Egertons, and undoubtedly the two families had many business dealings. As a matter of fact the Lupps were clockmakers; I have seen several clocks with the name of one of them on the dial and the label of Mathew Egerton, Jr., in the tall case.

Just when the first of the Lupps came to this country from their native Nieuweid-on-Rhine is uncertain. The name first appears on the baptismal rolls of the First Dutch Reformed Church, New Brunswick, in 1760, and after 1802 in the records of Christ Episcopal Church. Louis Lupp, the first to be identified as a silversmith, had his home and shop in Albany Street, near Peace Street, before the Revolution, and he is known to have died in 1800. Notices in the *New Brunswick Advertiser* and other papers of the day show that Henry Lupp, the oldest son, was in business in 1783, but he appears to have worked only as a silversmith. In 1784 he was town collector, and in 1787 an elder of the Dutch Reformed Church. Samuel, second of the family, was not long at the trade, because the rolls at Christ Church record his death in 1809, at twenty-one years of age. Peter, probably the most widely known and certainly the most versatile, was born in 1797 and died in 1827 at thirty years of age.

Spoons by Samuel V. Lupp

Local history in New Brunswick credits Peter Lupp with installing the first church clock in New Brunswick. It was placed in the tower of Christ Church about 1804 and kept the time of day for the population until it was removed in 1880. In the home of some of New Brunswick's and Middlesex County's older families may be found today silverware and clocks with the Lupp inscriptions.

Following the death of Peter Lupp in 1827 the business

was taken over by Elias Baker, who had a jewelry store for many years in Church Street. Lupp descendants continued prominent in the affairs of New Brunswick, although after 1840 they adopted the spelling Leupp. One of them, William H. Leupp, was a successful lawyer and became mayor of the city in 1845. The last one to bear the family name was William H. Leupp, a son, who died several years ago, when many of his papers on the family history were turned over to Rutgers University.

All of the Leupps, with the exception of Peter, used as their mark the family name prefixed by their initial. Peter's work was stamped with the letters "P.L." in a circle. The names of Louis, Peter, and Samuel have been found on the dials of tall face clocks, but they were silversmiths before they were clockmakers.

John Fitch, who first appeared in Trenton around 1776 from his native Connecticut, was an individual of varied attainments—he was by turn one of that city's first silversmiths, a clock repairer, gunsmith, and steamboat inventor. On silverware he used as his mark the head of a plumed knight in addition to his initial and last name. Examples of his work are rare and consist in the main of spoons. They are of excellent quality, but other activities left him little time to ply the trade.

Fitch was born in 1743. At the outbreak of the Revolution he became a lieutenant with the Connecticut troops, but ability shown as a gunsmith and armorer caused him to be sent to Trenton by Washington. There he had a place on King Street and made firearms for the Continental forces. When British troops made their attack in 1776 he was barely able to escape across the river into Pennsylvania and the enemy had to be content with the destruction of his shop.

Until the war ended Fitch devoted most of his efforts to the American cause. He then set out for the wild country of Ohio and Kentucky, where he acquired land. While on a voyage down the Ohio River he was captured by Indians and taken westward to Detroit before obtaining his freedom.

During all his travels over the vast unsettled country

Fitch came to have ideas about the need for transportation. There were no roads and the propelling of boats by oars on the broad rivers was a slow and tedious business. Those thoughts stayed with him after he returned to Pennsylvania and finally to Trenton. At about that time he spoke to a clergyman named the Reverend Nathaniel Irwin of his plans for a boat with an engine, and the minister showed him drawings of a stationary steam engine used for pumping at a copper mine in North Jersey.

The chance meeting with the Reverend Irwin gave Fitch the needed inspiration to go ahead with his experiments. He sought financial assistance from various sources without success. Pleas to Congress for the exclusive right to the results of his idea were refused. He even went to Washington and Benjamin Franklin in a futile effort to obtain backing. Finally, in 1786, the Legislature of New Jersey gave him the sole privilege for fourteen years to propel steam craft on the waters of the state and shortly afterward similar authority was given by Pennsylvania and Delaware.

The first steamboat built by Fitch, with three hundred dollars accumulated in subscriptions by friends, was tried out on the Delaware River below Trenton on July 27, 1786. The crude engine and arrangement of side paddle wheels was not brilliantly successful, but neither was it a failure. Fitch went back to his shop and put in a solid year of planning and constructing a second vessel.

When the improved craft was tried on the Delaware on August 22, 1787, members of the Constitutional Convention meeting at Princeton and other prominent men were on hand. Its best speed appears to have been about four miles an hour against the tide, but it was a steamboat, and as such it was years ahead of the craft that Robert Fulton was to try out in 1807 on the Hudson River. After Fitch proved that it could move without sails or oars and that it was not the dangerous contraption some people feared, he obtained backing for a company organized to run passenger boats. Several were built and one ran for years on the Potomac River.

After a few years, support for Fitch began to wane and

he went to France seeking aid. The French Revolution prevented any success in that direction and finally he shipped as an ordinary seaman to work his way back to America. During his absence others who had been working on his idea had succeeded in turning even his former supporters against him. For a time he tarried in Trenton and Philadelphia, but despairing of success, he went to Kentucky. Then, in the spring of 1798, he committed suicide and was buried in a pauper's grave at Bardstown in that state.

Belated recognition has been given to Fitch's genius. In 1887, just one hundred years after the successful trial of his first steamboat, the Connecticut Legislature placed a bronze tablet in the State Capitol. Shortly afterward the citizens of Bardstown reinterred his remains in the village square and erected a memorial with $15,000 appropriated by Congress. In 1921 the State of New Jersey placed a marker on the east bank of the Delaware River, opposite the spot where Fitch tried out his craft.

Another Trenton silversmith was Abner Reeder, a native Jerseyman, who was destined to learn his trade in Philadelphia and spend a considerable part of his life in Pennsylvania before returning to his own state.

Reeder was born in 1766 at Ewing, in what is now Mercer County, but which was then Hunterdon County. His parents were John and Hannah Marchone Reeder, both early settlers of Ewing. Abner was tenth in a family of sixteen children and after a common schooling was apprenticed to a silversmith in Philadelphia. By 1793 he had become a member of the firm of M'Fee & Reeder at 38 North Front Street, that city. The partnership was dissolved three years later and until 1800 Reeder continued in business alone at the same address.

It seems that Reeder had other talents than as a silversmith. He became a landowner and in 1796 married Hannah Wilkinson, daughter of Colonel John Wilkinson, a soldier in the Revolution and a prominent Pennsylvanian. Among the silver definitely attributed to him is a four-piece

Abner B. Reeder sugar bowl

tea service made in 1796 for Rebecca Howard, who at the time was a member of a well-known Philadelphia family. The sugar bowl now is in the possession of the Colonial Dames of New York by presentation from a descendant.

In 1800 Reeder removed to Trenton and for years maintained a shop in State Street. In a short time he became a prominent figure and a man of affairs. When the State Bank was organized in 1804 he was one of the five directors and afterward was named postmaster. In 1824 he aided in the city's reception to Lafayette on the occasion of the patriotic Frenchman's revisit to the United States.

Death came to Reeder in October, 1841, at the age of seventy-five years and he was buried in the Presbyterian cemetery at Ewing, where his wife was laid beside him eight years later.

Aaron Lane, listed as a silversmith and clockmaker in Elizabethtown and whose work is identified only by his initials on spoons and other pieces found today, was a prominent citizen from 1780 until after 1815. He was born in New York City in 1753 and had learned his trade before going to Elizabethtown, where he set up a shop on Water Street, now Elizabeth Avenue. The building is still standing as a part of the Egenolf Day Nursery.

Around 1793 Lane's silverware and clocks were much in demand, but he was active in town affairs and gradually retired from business. He is recorded as one of the managers of the Elizabethtown and New Brunswick church lottery authorized in 1786. An advertisement in the *New York Gazeteer* of June 16, 1788, stated that it was "for the purpose of finishing a building erected by the Presbyterian church congregation of Elizabethtown."

From 1790 until 1795 he was a village alderman. He was an active church worker, indicated by a record showing him as chairman of a town committee formed in 1813 "to suppress by all lawful means the growng profanation of the Lord's Day." Again, in 1814, we find that he was one of a committee of citizens authorized by the town fathers to supervise the raising of $2,500 to meet expenses arising from the War of 1812. He died in New York City on October 24, 1819. A son, Andrew, carried on in his father's footsteps.

A descendant of one of Elizabethtown's pioneer families was a leading silversmith there in the early 1800s. He was Elias Darby, who became the community's fourth mayor, from 1855 to 1860, after he had maintained a shop for many years at the northeast corner of Jefferson Avenue and East Jersey Street. He was a son of Elias Darby, Sr., who died in 1798, and Sally Darby, who died in 1839, both of whom are buried in the Presbyterian Church cemetery.

The junior Darby learned his trade from Aaron Lane and in New York prior to setting up his own shop. He used his initials "E.D." on articles of silver and the mark identifies spoons, creamers, and a coffeepot possessed by Elizabeth families. The bellows and anvil from his shop are in the collection of the Union County Historical Society.

Another early silversmith in Elizabethtown was Benjamin Halstead. Apparently learning his craft and working in New York for a time, he moved to New Jersey in 1766. He advertised for the first time in the *New York Gazette* on September 26 of that year, as follows:

> Benjamin and Mathias (a brother) Halstead take this method to acquaint the public that they have now set up their business in Elizabethtown, nearly opposite Joseph Jelf's, merchant, where they propose to carry on as gold and silversmiths in all branches.

The somewhat lengthy notice for those times goes on to say that Benjamin Halstead had followed the same business for some time in New York "to the satisfaction of his employers and hopes that his former customers there and in the country will not forget him." The promise was made that orders would be obeyed on the shortest notice, "as we propose to make work of all qualities (prices accordingly) and hope that our employers will not expect the best of work for the meanest prices."

Mathias apparently did not tarry long in the business. He was soon advertising for sale "a few silversmith's tools which he will sell cheap for cash, viz: Forging, polishing, hollowing and bouge hammers; piercing, riffling and common files; fine Turkey oil slips, and Bohemian polishing stones; double aqua fortis stone, coin, half coin and emery flour."

A communion service made by Halstead in 1806 is owned by Trinity Church and another is owned by the Old First Church (Presbyterian), both in Newark. They were exhibited several years ago by the Newark Museum, along with a silver tablespoon bearing the mark of Benjamin Cleveland. Cleveland was the son of William Cleveland, a pioneer Newark clockmaker and ancestor of Grover Cleveland. Benjamin Cleveland is recorded in early histories of Newark as having been in business in 1792. He was born in Newark in 1767 and died there in 1837.

Another who plied his trade in Newark was Cyrus Durand. He was born in 1787 and was apprenticed to a silversmith as a young boy. After serving his time, he set up in business for himself and when the demand developed for jewelry, he became one of the first in the field. After 1850 he relinquished active management of the firm to several of his workmen and thereafter the firm was known as Durand & Co.

The firm of Hayes & Cotton had a silver and goldsmith shop in Newark around 1830. Articles of jewelry also were made.

One of the early craftsmen in Morristown was John Dickerson, a New Englander, who was located there during at least a part of the Revolutionary War period. While Washington and his army were encamped in and around the town for the winters of 1777 and 1779, it was one of the most important centers in the colonies and Dickerson undoubtedly was busy at his trade despite the hard times.

For a period of several years, beginning in 1783, Daniel Van Voorhis was a silversmith in Princeton, as indicated by an advertisement in the *New Jersey Gazette* for February 5 of that year. He was born at Oyster Bay, Long Island, on August 30, 1751, and is believed to have learned his trade in Philadelphia, where he advertised in the *Pennsylvania Gazette* of May 6, 1782, that he had removed from Market Street to the west side of Front Street.

During his time in Princeton he is known to have made many pieces of silver. Included are two sugar tongs, one made for General Morris, with a bill of sale bearing his signature dated 1783, now in the Museum of the City of New York. Other known pieces are trays, ladles, several tea sets, shoe buckles, and a basin. Several Indian arm-bands have been found bearing his mark, one of which is in the collection of Dr. R. P. Burke of Montgomery, Alabama. It was found in 1933 in an old Indian grave on the Old Creek townsite of Tuckabache in that state, and bears the date 1789.

In 1786 Van Voorhis was located in New York under the partnership name of Voorhis & Cooley at 27 Hanover Square. During the next two decades he was listed from half a dozen different addresses in that city, in 1791 as a partner of Garret Schenck, a cousin and in 1798 with his son, Charles. The younger man died in 1805 and soon afterward Van Voorhis entered the United States Customs service at New York as a weigher. He died in Brooklyn in 1824.

Reference is made earlier in the chapter to the absence of native pewterers of the colonial period in New Jersey. The author has searched over pretty much the entire state without results. I learn from Ledlie I. Laughlin of Princeton, one of the foremost collectors of that ware, that he has been no more successful. As a matter of fact, he is the authority for the statement that New Jersey and Delaware are the only two of the original thirteen colonies where no trace has been found of such local craftsmen.

New York and Philadelphia were important centers in those days, within comparatively easy reach, and it is probable that pewterers in those cities and the Middletown area of Connecticut covered New Jersey fairly well by means of their peddlers' carts.

Practically all of the American pewter turned up in New Jersey—and there has been a considerable amount—bears the marks of New York, Philadelphia, or Connecticut makers. Numerous pieces of English origin also have been found and thus it is hardly likely that there was any actual shortage when it was in demand. It is fair to assume that the cruder pewterware that has been discovered was reworked from articles worn by constant use and that those Jerseymen who did the work did not even bother with identifying marks for what probably was undertaken through economic necessity.

New Jersey's position as one of the middle colonies has made it surprisely fertile ground for "finds" of pewterware despite the absence of craftsmen of that trade within her borders. It accounts for the turning up of pieces after the Dutch style from around New York, of the German plates and porringers from Pennsylvania, and of some from New England.

During a three-year period while the Revolution was in progress New Jersey was a refuge for one of the famous pewter craftsmen. The *New Jersey Journal* of May 31, 1780, carried an advertisement of Francis Bassett, who "acquaints the public that he carries on the 'Pewter's Business at Horse-Neck, Essex County." Undoubtedly he was the famous craftsman from New York and the fortunes of war that placed the British in possession of that city made it more convenient for him to seek temporary haven in New Jersey. During the same time his brother, Frederick, worked in Hartford, Connecticut.

On June 14, 1780, the *New Jersey Journal* carried the following notice:

The subscriber acquaints the public that he carries on the Peweterer's Business at Horse-Neck, Essex County, near Mr. Caleb Hetfield's, where he makes and mends all sorts of pewter, such as plates, bason, tankers, court pots, &c., &c, provided they bring him old pewter.

Francis Bassett

Another Bassett record found is dated April 3, 1782 and reads:

> The subscriber takes this method to acquaint the public that he has removed from Horse-Neck to Crane's Town, opposite Mr. William Crane's, where he continues to make and mend all sort of pewter ware, with the provision they bring old silver.
> N. B. said Bassett gives cash for old pewter

The Horse-Neck referred to was forerunner of Caldwell; Crane Town is present-day Montclair. The Crane house was located at Valley Road and Claremont Avenue, Montclair, and Washington stayed there on several occasions.

The final record in the *New Jersey Journal* dates from May 14, 1793, when Bassett advertised for sale "that very pleasantly situated small place whereon Mr. Garrett Roorbach now lives at Gotham, near Aquackanock bridge. For terms apply to the subscriber in Crane Town, who also has for sale one horse, two mares, a riding sleigh &x."

It is likely that Bassett returned to New York shortly after the British evacuated. He died early in 1800 and his will, approved April 24 in that year, was dated September 21, 1798.

The beginning of jewelry making in New Jersey dates back to the first years of the nineteenth century. As a matter of fact it was really a further development of the gold and silversmith trades, brought about as a result of improved living conditions and a demand for more ornamentation on the part of the fair sex and even the men.

Epaphras Hinsdale, a silversmith, was the pioneer of the state's jewelry industry. In 1801 he was doing business in a little shop on the east side of Broad Street, near Lafayette Street, in Newark. Apparently he did not want for customers, because in accounts of the city's history for that period it is remarked that it was "quite the fashion for ladies of means to drive up to Hinsdale's in their carriages to inspect his wares."

Around 1805 Hinsdale was operating a factory and employed six hands to make the brooches and other articles of adornment that were popular at the time. Soon afterward he formed a partnership with a James Taylor. In Newark, and subsequently in New York, to which the firm moved in 1807, it produced various articles with the mark "T & H" in a rectangle.

In 1820 the firm of Taylor & Baldwin started in Franklin Street, Newark, and by 1836 there were fifty jewelers and four jewelry establishments listed in the city directory. The name of Baldwin long continued to be identified with the industry and as late as 1850 was represented by S. M. Baldwin & Co. In 1860 there were twenty-seven manufacturing jewelry houses in Newark. The city has retained its place through the years, so that it long has been regarded as a center of the industry in this country, with nearly one hundred and fifty establishments in 1970 turning out millions of dollars' worth of products annually.

Other pioneer jewelry firms of Newark were Durand & Co., Carter, Hawkins & Dodd, Enos Richardson & Co., and Paxson & Hayes. They achieved superiority in the manufacture and designing of rings, bracelets, chains, and other articles of adornment that contained as high as fifty percent gold. Gradually they overcame the prejudice in New York, Boston, and Philadelphia against domestic jewelry and their jewelry successfully competed with importations from Paris and London.

7

Jersey Glass and Glassmakers

The beginning of successful glass blowing in this country goes back well over two hundred years to the southern part of New Jersey. It was in 1738 that Casper Wistar, a German, began erection of a "glass house" near what is now Allowaystown in Salem County, and in the following year he started production of first, window lights, then bottles and various other delicately colored and shaped articles, which are among the rarest of objects sought today by collectors.

There were earlier ventures at glassmaking on American soil, but none of them lasted long or achieved more than a meager output. The initial effort was at the Jamestown, Virginia, colony in 1608 and apparently was short-lived. The second was also at Jamestown, in 1621, lasting until 1625, but its output was limited apparently to crudely shaped bottles and beads for trade with the Indians. There are records of attempts at the manufacture of glass in Salem, Massachusetts, around 1638, in New York by 1655, and in Pennsylvania along Perkiomen Creek about 1707, but in none of those instances can it be said that there was any permanency.

Wistar started his venture, almost a quarter of a century before Steigel, at Manheim, in neighboring Pennsylvania.

He landed in Philadelphia in 1717 from his native Germany and obtained work in a button factory. That undertaking was a success and after the elapse of a decade he had acquired sufficient means to buy land in Salem County.

Late in 1739 Wistar's project had advanced to the stage that his glass house was ready to start production. In the meanwhile he had arranged to pay for the transportation of four expert glass blowers from Holland. By the terms of an agreement with them, he was to have the sole right to their services in the art of glassmaking. He in turn offered to provide land, fuel, servants, food, and materials, and to advance money for their support and give them one-third of the profits.

Undoubtedly the Dutch influence was responsible for the early examples of so-called Wistarberg ware. In the beginning he made only window glass, in response to a growing demand at a period when larger and better dwellings were being constructed in all parts of the colonies. Bottles also were turned out soon after and the two products in combination made possible the foundation for a sound business structure that was a monument to his unusual ability.

Soon the Wistar factory was turning out a variety of articles as the skill of its workers increased and the market for its wares widened. They included dishes, drinking vessels, bowls, pitchers, pickle jars, snuff containers, scent and drug bottles, lamp glasses, vases, measures, mustard pots, and sundry other objects. Glass balls of various sizes were made, to be used as stoppers.

The Wistar works prospered to the extent that in 1748 German workmen were brought over, with the result that an even greater variety of articles was made and the range of colors was increased. Besides the green of many hues most associated with Wistarberg, there were pieces of turquoise blue and of amber, in addition to the clear white. A peculiarity by which certain types of Wistar products are most readily identified even to this day was achieved by placing a second layer of glass over a portion of an article

Bowl with ball cover. COURTESY THE METROPOLITAN MUSEUM OF ART

for added decoration. Another characteristic was a large thread, or cord, of glass spirally wrapped around the neck of a bottle or pitcher, or at the top of a mug.

Casper Wistar died in 1752 in Philadelphia. He had

South Jersey pitcher— Wistarberg. COURTESY THE MET-
ROPOLITAN MUSEUM OF ART

continued in the button-making industry and managed the
financial end of the glass works. Production details were
left largely to his Dutch and German employees. He
brought his son, Richard, up in the business and the younger
man, after the parent's death, greatly expanded operations.

At the outbreak of the Revolution the fires were drawn
at the Wistar works and they never returned to prewar
activities. Richard Wistar died in 1781 at Rahway. The

older workmen had for the most part either passed away or started other glass houses, and in 1781, the year Richard died, the works were abandoned.

Authentic pieces of Wistarberg are very rare. As a matter of fact it is very difficult to say that a particular article of glassware is of that origin. In view of the similarity between early American and European glass of the same period, much of it that is ascribed to this country undoubtedly was imported. Then, too, attempts in recent years at reproduction have added to the uncertainty.

While the Wistar factory was in successful operation for close to half a century, there was little if any competition from other Jersey ventures. Eventually his workers broke away and, once the movement began, numerous glass houses were started . There was very little capital in back of them and living conditions for the workmen were far from favorable. Frame buildings to cover the fires and the glass blowers were erected in isolated wooded sections, where timber for fuel was readily obtainable, and shacks for the employees were close by.

Eventually places were set up along tidal waters for greater ease in transporting fuel and materials and in forwarding products to New York and Philadelphia. Even so, they remained for the most part not readily accessible and company stores were maintained where "shin-plasters" received for pay were redeemable in merchandise.

In 1834 there were eleven glass factories in the southern part of the state. There were two each at Glassboro, Millville, and Waterford. Others were located at Jackson's Woods, Malaga, Pleasant Mills, and Port Elizabeth. The United States census of 1840 shows that by then there was an increase to twenty-eight establishments, and in 1843 agitation arose for a tariff on imported glass products to protect home industry.

When the so-called Sandwich or pressed-glass period came around 1826, New Jersey glassmakers were faced with competition from outside the state. It was brought to this

A group of Jersey glassware. COURTESY THE METRO-
POLITAN MUSEUM OF ART

country by Deming Jarvis, an Englishman. He formed the
Boston & Sandwich Glass Company for the purpose of
making the type of glassware that already was familiar in
England. The more modern methods and mass production
were too much for the Jersey glass blowers and they steadily
lost ground in filling the demand for table and decorative
ware, although the lead was maintained in bottles and druggists' supplies. Efforts to imitate the Sandwich glass were
not successful.

As the years went on, markets abroad were gradually cut
off, a result of the increasing flow of exports from the
Sandwich works. Even New Jersey homes came to have the
glass plates, cups, and other articles brought in by New
England peddlers. That is the reason why so much old
Sandwich glass has been found in this state. It includes the
beautiful shades of canary, transparent purple, apple green,

Goblet with red base. COURTESY THE METROPOLITAN MUSEUM OF ART

Amber and white pitcher. COURTESY THE METROPOLI-
TAN MUSEUM OF ART

opal, and the ambers of the colored glass first made at the
Sandwich factory in 1835.

The first glass house in Glassboro, the second in South
Jersey, was erected by seven brothers named Stanger, after
the Wistar factory, where they had worked, was closed in

1781. Tax assessment records in Greenwich Township for that year bear the name of Solomon Stanger as owner of land on which stood the factory. His brothers, Daniel, Adam, Christian, Francis, Peter, and Philip, were taxed on dwellings.

In 1783 Thomas Carpenter and Samuel Tonkin bought out Francis, Peter, and Philip. One year later Solomon sold his interest to Colonel Thomas Heston for three hundred and thirty pounds, gold and silver. By 1784-85 the enterprise was run as Tonkin & Carpenter, and in 1786 as Heston & Carpenter. Apparently the Stangers were not good financiers and lost through debt.

Heston & Carpenter added flint glassware and window glass to the original bottle line of the Stangers. The factory came to be known as the Olive Glass Works and passed through various hands until purchased in 1824 by Jeremiah Foster, who merged it with the Harmony Glass Works.

The Harmony Glass Works was started in 1813 by some workmen who left the Olive factory when Carpenter died. Among them were several of the Stangers and a John Rink. He lived in Philadelphia and was the financial manager, attending to the purchase of supplies and sale of products until his death in 1823.

The *Village Herald* of Woodbury for July 31, 1823, carried an advertisement offering for sale a dwelling house and five acres, as follows:

> The Harmony Glass Works consisting of a large glass house, mill house, packing house, pot house, storehouse, several dwelling, etc., comprising a complete estate well worthy the attention of persons disposed to engage in the glass business.

Lewis Stanger, apparently a son of one of the seven brothers, who had been active in the Harmony works, withdrew in 1834 and a Thomas H. Whitney got control. In 1837 he bought out the others and with Samuel, a brother, formed the firm of Whitney Brothers, which continued until 1882. The company incorporated in 1887 as the Whitney Glass Works and in 1918 was absorbed by the Owens Bottle Company. The Whitneys were grandsons of Colonel Thomas Heston and advertised as having been established in 1776, although that is not borne out by the record and probably was intended to refer back to the beginnings of the works in which their kinsman was interested.

The Whitneys made hollow ware and bottles that were sold all over the country. The bottles included Plantation Bitters, Fisch Bitters, Dutchman, Indian Queen, Log Cabin, and Warner's Safe Bottles. Others were Tippecanoe, Bunker Hill Pickle, Wishart's Pine Tree Cordial, and Perrine Apple Ginger bottles.

Whitney Brothers bottles. COURTESY THE METROPOLITAN MUSEUM OF ART

Bridgeton bottles. COURTESY THE METROPOLITAN MU-
SEUM OF ART

After Lewis Stanger got out of the Harmony works in
1834 he, a brother, Jacob, and a son, George, started a
plant nearby. It was called the Lewisville and Temperanceville Works, because they would employ only abstainers as
workmen. In 1841 they failed and Whitney Brothers took
over. Soon afterward the Whitney brothers took into the
firm Woodward Warrick, who had married a sister. The
firm continued as Whitney & Warrick until 1864 and then,
with a Thomas Stanger, carried on until 1883.

The first glassmaking venture was started in Camden
County, about 1800, at a place later called Clementon.
Jonathan Haines built a factory and was aided by a William
Stanger in the production of bottles. After failure in 1817
or 1818, it was bought in by a Samuel Clementon and oper-
ated as a window-glass works for several years. Until it was

Olive green bottle. COURTESY THE METROPOLITAN MUSEUM OF ART

abandoned in 1825, it was known as the Clementon Glass Works.

There is no record of a glass factory in Bridgeton until 1836. In that year John P. Buck and Nathaniel Stratton erected a "house" and produced bottles until 1841. In that year Buck died and John G. Rosenbaum purchased an interest. The works were taken over in 1846 by Joel Bodine, who was the sole owner until David Potter was taken in around 1857. The partners were producing bottles of light-green glass until 1867. The factory was last operated in 1870, under the name of the Cohansay Glass Manufacturing Company.

The Capewell Glass Works was built at Camden in 1841 by John and James G. Capewell and John Bamfort. Later they changed the name to The Excelsior Glass Works and produced flint and cut glass of good quality until the venture failed in 1857.

A second glass works in Camden County was erected on Cooper's Creek in 1850 by Coffin & Hay. It produced window glass, for the most part, and was known as the Sasockson Glass Works.

One of the earliest recorded glass factories in Burlington County was erected at Green Bank, Washington Township, in 1840 by William Coffin, Sr., and operated by his son, John H. Coffin. It was known as Wapler's Glass Works in 1850, and after having been shut down for several years was rented in 1857 to strikers from Glassboro only to be abandoned in a short time. In 1869 a new factory was built on the site by Scott & Rapp to make flint glass, including lamp shades, buttons, stars, and cut-glass ware.

Samuel Crowley built a glass works in 1851 on the banks of the Mullica River below Batsto. He called the place Crowleytown and made bottles and druggists' wares. After a year it was taken over by New York men as the Atlantic Glass Works and later operated by Burling Brothers until abandoned in 1858. In the same year Crowley started a small glass house at Bulltown on Bull Creek, two miles from the Mullica River, and it continued until 1870.

About 1838-40, when Coffin was beginning at Green Bank, the Millford Glass Works was set up at Milford (Millford) in Burlington County by Matthias Zimmerman and others. In 1852 it was controlled by Lippencott, Wisham & Co. In addition to druggists' ware, the factory turned out the Jennie Lind alabaster bottle.

Medford, in Burlington County, had its first glass works in 1842. It started with production of window glass and by 1860, as Cochran's Glass Works, it was turning out fancy tableware. One article was a squatty decanter-shaped bottle in blue, showing spiral turning when held to the light.

Among the early Camden County glass enterprises was the Brooklyn Glass Works started at Old Brooklyn in 1831 by John Marshall, an Englishman. He was aided by Frederick Stanger, a son-in-law, and at one time employed as many as twenty glass blowers and sixty to eighty wood cutters. The factory had closed prior to burning in 1855.

Thomas W. Stanger, a cousin of Frederick, built a "house" at Williamstown on the Brooklyn road in 1848 and called it the Isabella Glass Works after his daughter. He made the Yankee Quart Flasks, among other products. After his death in 1857, Clayton Tice carried on until 1868.

In 1835, four years after the Brooklyn Glass Works started, William Nichols and several others from Squankum founded the Free Will Glass Works at Williamstown and made bottles.

The first glass factory was started at Port Elizabeth, Cumberland County, in 1799, by James Lee and a group of Philadelphians to make window glass. In 1810, the original owners sold the property and it passed through various hands as the Eagle Glass Works.

Cape May County had the Dennisville Glass Company in 1836, as its first contribution to the industry. It was located on Dennis Creek and for the most part made only window glass. Among the backers were Nathaniel Holmes and Samuel Matthews.

A "Lazy Susan"

At Estellville, in Atlantic County, John H. Scott started a glass factory in 1825. It passed to his son, Daniel, in 1834 and in 1844 eighty glass blowers and cutters were employed. By 1868 the firm had changed to Getzinger & Rosenbaum and a year prior to closing in 1876 the business was purchased by Alexander H. Sharp.

Christian L. Stanger and others built the first glass "house" at Malage, Gloucester County, in 1814. It was taken over later by Rosenbaum and then by the Whitney brothers, who ran it for thirty years for the making of window glass.

The Marshallville Glass Works were located at Tuckahoe, in Gloucester County, about 1810. Hollow ware was made at first and then window glass, but the owners are not known.

At Clayton, in the same county, Jacob P. Fisler and Benjamin Becket began the Fislerville Glass Works in 1850. The following year Becket sold out to Edward Bacon and the firm continued until Bacon died in 1856, after which Fisler transferred his interest to John M. Moore. As Moore Brothers, the factory operated until 1880, although advertisements in Philadelphia papers continued to show the Fislerville Glass Works as producers of druggists' wares, perfumers' glass, and wine, mineral, and other bottles. The Jennie Lind bottle, so eagerly sought by collectors, was also made at this factory.

The single early glass factory of record in Warren County was at Columbia, in Knowlton Township, near the mouth of the Paulinskill. It was established in 1812 by Francis Myerhoff as the Columbia Glass Works. Workmen from Holland at first made hollow ware and later window glass. The sand was obtained from a pond bottom near the Sussex County line. Some of Myerhoff's associates were John Beck, William Lillianthal, and William Heyberger.

The manufacture of glass products was begun first in the northeastern part of the state when George Dummer, Joseph K. Milmer, and William G. Bell established the

Green and ruby vase. COURTESY THE METROPOLITAN MUSEUM OF ART

Jersey City Glass Works in 1824. Dummer was still running the business in 1850 and making flint and cut-glass tumblers, jars, and vases. He was succeeded by Reed & Moulds, who sold the factory in 1860 to the New Jersey Sugar Refining Company, and the glass works were abandoned.

H. O'Neil founded the Jersey City Flint Glass Works in

South Jersey pitcher—milk white. COURTESY THE METROPOLITAN MUSEUM OF ART

1861 and made plain, pressed, molded, and cut-flint colored glassware.

Probably the most widely known and collected of our early glass is so-called milk glass. Although it was made as far back as 1830, shortly after Phineas C. Dummer of Jersey City and others had been issued patents on the production of pressed glassware, public demand was lacking until the craze for complete table settings took hold in the 1870s.

Milk white glass has come to be reproduced to such an extent that it is very risky to buy any of it as the genuine thing without knowing its history. The average collector, or casual buyer, will be taking a plain gamble otherwise.

The difference between opaque, opal, opalescent, and milk white glass has been explained at length over the years and yet it is not understood. All four types come under the general classification of pressed ware. Each one has its serious collectors and admirers, but milk glass far outranks the others in popularity. It is best described as that through which nothing at all is seen.

Besides the matched pieces of a set, original milk glass is to be found in animal covered dishes, such as the hen, swan, horse, kitten, and owl. Other pieces are the classic fluted bowls, as well as the S-border, one-thousand-eye border and the Gothic-style plates. Often they may show remnants of painting or gilt, as a reminder of the days when they were threaded with ribbon and hung on the wall.

Some of the finest old lamps were made, at least in part, of milk glass, as were the dolphin candlesticks. There were dresser sets of milk glass, as well as clock cases, match boxes, water fonts, souvenir hatchets, and numerous other articles reproduced these days in response to popular demand.

Although the art of making paperweights goes back in glass history at least until 1840, those produced right here in New Jersey at the works of Whitall, Tatum & Co. during the period from 1863 until 1910 or later are tops on

South Jersey globe. COURTESY THE METROPOLITAN MU-
SEUM OF ART

the list of most collectors.

The Millville Rose, so named after the town where the firm was located, is rated best among the many designs of paperweights definitely attributed to a group of its workmen. Beginning about 1905, it was the accomplishment of Ralph Barber, who took several years to perfect his creation. From that point on, as others became proficient, changes were made so that the deep red rose often became pink, white, or yellow.

Most of the rose weights, both with and without stems, were hand blown, with the flower upright. A few have it tilted and occasionally it is in a horizontal position. It is usual for these weights to rest on a heavy circular foot, with the rose realistically nestled in natural-looking leaves.

The making of paperweights at the Whitall, Tatum works started with the establishing of a wooden mold department. The first ones were crude by comparison with those from Europe, but the art was just getting started in this country and experience was on the short side. The earliest paperweights at Millville were made with a lily bloom. It was not well designed and the few colors were not well selected. About the same time appeared the fountain, devil's swirl, and other plain, flat types.

Improved design and craft skill were rapid. Less than a decade passed before Whitall, Tatum and other glass houses in South Jersey and around the country were making paperweights that were greatly improved over the first efforts. What are believed by many collectors to be the best of the lily design were made in the 1870s, as were also the upright eagles, dogs, horses, potted flowers, and boats.

Barber stood out as one of a group of expert craftsmen at the Millville works around 1880. Others included Emil Stanger, who was descended from the first glass workers brought to this country in 1739. Then there were Marcus Kuntz, John Rhulander, and Michael Kane.

Collectors of pitchers who decide to concentrate on those of glass will find very soon that the variety of style, size,

Blown glass pitcher. COURTESY THE METROPOLITAN MUSEUM OF ART

and other details are many. Jersey craftsmen not only pioneered in glass. They began by making window glass and bottles in the mid-eighteenth century. Soon they were turning out pitchers and almost every other article of utilitarian or decorative value for which there was a demand.

Pitchers have been made over the years from blown, pressed, pattern, and cut glass. Then there have been those of the so-called milk, frosted, ruby, and other colored glass. Pieces after the "South Jersey tradition" come first in the jargon of collectors, because the pioneer workers moved about and taught their craft in many areas.

It may be well to outline the order of types, or styles, to which pitchers and other glass articles have passed since colonial times. Arrangement according to age is best when identification by association with a particular factory or glass house is not possible.

First, there were pitchers of blown glass styled after the Continental and British products. They gave birth to the distinctive designs and decorations of Jersey origin.

Next came the patterned molded glass of the 1760s, followed by the blown three-patterned molded glass, his-

Ribbed glass bowl

torical and pictorial glass. The early pressed and lacy glass
dates from the 1820s.

As glass making passed from one method to another, the
earlier procedures were never completely abandoned. This
accounts for the fact that pitchers, as well as other tableware, in popular patterns dating from the 1840s and 1850s
are considered to be early pressed pattern glass.

South Jersey blown glass

Most of the glass pitchers made in New Jersey during the latter half of the eighteenth century ranged from three to five or six inches in height. Regardless of size, they were distinguished by a short neck in proportion to the body. The earliest South Jersey type in the Metropolitan Museum is a brilliant deep green. The short neck is threaded with ruby glass and a lily pad is superimposed on the body.

Another pitcher in the Metropolitan's collection of old Jersey glass is aquamarine in color, with a rare combination of applied and superimposed decoration, threaded neck, wavy band around the base, and crimped foot. A ball of clear glass is the stopper, except for the small spout allowing liquid to pass.

The proper identification of early glass is so difficult and risky that I have asked the Metropolitan Museum in New York for permission to use pictures from its own collection of the so-called South Jersey glassware as illustrations.

8

Workers in Pottery and Chinaware

*P*ottery and tile making in New Jersey go far back
into its history. Even before the white man's time,
the Indians who roamed the region had discovered that the
soil in certain localities was suited for the fashioning of
crude vessels or containers, but they were fragile at best
and the only examples found have been fragments.

There is no definite record of when the early settlers first
attempted pottery making. It must have followed soon
after the Dutch from New Amsterdam began trading with
the Indians. The remains of a kiln thought to be from those
times was found in the 1920s a few miles outside of South
Amboy. It is likely that there were others equally old of
which no trace remains.

Court records reveal existence of the first potteries in the
southern part of the state around 1684. One of them was
set up by a Daniel Coxe, of whom I shall say more later.

Redware and a bit later stoneware were the earliest forms
of pottery in the state's colonial era. With a soil at hand
suited for the purpose and a ready demand from all the
colonies, it was quite natural that the making of earthenware
was important. In time the art of fine china manufacture
came to be known and down to the present day the state
has continued to be a leader.

Redware is distinguished by a transparent glaze that is really glass. It has a slightly yellow tinge and whenever the color of a piece of redware is other than red, it indicates an impurity in the glaze. This accounts for the shades of green sometimes found when copper oxide was added, or brown resulting from the use of powdered manganese.

Other colors found in old redware were caused by slip decoration. An entire piece may have been immersed in a liquid clay of cream or other hue, or perhaps the slip was applied in designs or spots. Glaze was then applied over the slip to make a piece watertight, as contrasted to the unglazed rough redware. The glaze served to accentuate colors and produced a shiny surface.

During its long production redware changed very little in either style or shade, which is one reason for the difficulty in determining age or producer. Generally speaking, the pieces produced prior to 1800 are taller, thinner, and with more straight lines than the shorter and rounder articles that came later.

The early redware was individualistic in character and independent in both form and design compared to the later product that was less carefully and even mass made in an effort to meet competition from abroad.

Redware gradually gave way before the latter-nineteenth-century inroads by china and other ware that came into being through employing new techniques. Its last stand may be seen in the fields of brickmaking, flower pots, and jars for sundry uses.

Stoneware is best described as a product of clay, with a hard or vitrified body. It is considered an intermediate between earthenware and porcelain. It differs from redware in that it is not porous and from porcelain in that it is not translucent. It is made from a single clay, usually gray or buff in color, whereas porcelain is made from a fine white clay, to which flint and feldspar have been added. On the other hand, stoneware is the product of firing at a higher temperature than earthenware, with the result that it is much stronger and not porous when it becomes vitrified and cold. Salt-glazed stoneware was produced by throwing common salt into the kiln when firing of the ware was nearly finished and this has remained a favorite method for making crocks, jugs, and many other types of containers.

There are several areas over the state where clay deposits exist, and from the beginning they have served as a source of raw material. Probably the most important is that district in and around Woodbridge, South River, South Amboy, and Sayreville on the Raritan River. Another is outside of Trenton, and a third along the lower reaches of the Delaware River.

The first pottery ware was made in a very crude fashion. The Indian custom of firing the hand-worked clay in open fires was improved upon by the use of kilns, but they were not very substantial at best. Usually they were of stone, with an inner recess or space for the ware to be placed. The space in between was filled with fuel for the fire and because wood was used for fuel at first, just as in the case of glassmaking, the kilns were located in the midst of forest areas and the clay transported to them.

The method of preparing the clay for use was simple in comparison to the elaborate procedure of the present day. The raw material was thrown into a pit and churned with a paddle, after which it was separated into chunks for cutting through and through by means of a thin wire or piece of wood held by workers. This last-mentioned process removed the pebbles and other foreign matter until finally the clay was ready for working, by hand or on a potter's wheel. The articles were then placed in a kiln and fired for varying periods of time.

The earliest pottery of authentic court record, as previously mentioned, was founded by Dr. Daniel Coxe, one of the first governors of West Jersey. It was established near Burlington about 1684 and was operated by his agent, John Tatham, and a son, Daniel Coxe, Jr. The owner is said never to have come to America, but in a letter dated

1688 he wrote of having helped to found a town, apparently in the vicinity of Cape May, at an expense of three thousand pounds, for development of the whaling industry.

Another document left by Dr. Coxe, who was physician at the Court of Charles II, apparently was an inventory of the Burlington tract, comprising 95,000 acres, to which he held title until 1692. During that time affairs were administered from a place called Coxehall and among the ventures was the pottery. Of it he wrote:

> I have erected a pottery at Burlington for white and chiney ware, a greate quantity to ye value of 1200 li have already been made and vended in ye country, neighbor colonies and ye Islands of Barbadoes and Jamaica, where they are in great request. I have two houses and kilns with all the necessary implements, diverse workmen and other servants. Have expended there about 2000 li.

Burlington County court records have been found indicating a dispute involving the Coxe property about 1685, which goes to prove that it must have been established somewhat earlier. A James Budd was plaintiff and Edward Randall, a potter, the defendant. The action was for payment of two hundred pounds for failure to discharge certain duties to Randall's satisfaction. William Winn, another potter, was one of the witnesses.

None of the pottery from Dr. Coxe's venture has been positively identified and the present owners of land where it is thought to have been actually located have refused to permit digging for trace of it. In 1692 the last of the property, including the pottery, was sold for about nine thousand pounds.

It is a pity that more details of the other early potteries have not come down to us, but historians of those days could not foresee that the time would come when collectors would cherish such data. Undoubtedly there were numerous ventures that sprang up and prospered awhile before encountering financial or other trouble. There is casual mention here and there among old deeds and other documents of such undertakings and of workmen from English potteries who came to this country with ideas, formulas, and designs for improving quality.

All during the colonial period England was not anxious to have competition to her own manufactures and was not at all helpful in the starting of enterprises. She was intent mainly on getting materials from the colonies, and clay was one of them. Wedgewood and the other English potters wanted the markets in America for themselves and all the better ware was imported. It was only the cruder articles that were made here, because they were in demand among the people who could not afford better.

The Revolution brought about a change that gave great impetus to the demand for native stoneware. As the colonists stopped buying imports from England, they were obliged to turn to homemade goods. Stoneware crocks and pitchers did not measure up to Queen's ware or Wedgewood's products, but they proved to be about as serviceable. The supply from New Jersey potteries became so essential that they were operated during all of the war, even when most other enterprises were at a standstill.

In Revolutionary times a few bricks were made at a small plant on Assunpink Creek, near Trenton. There also is record of brick making from 1780 to 1801 at Hamilton Square and a little later at Maiden Head, now Lawrenceville.

The first potter around Flemington was Samuel Hill. In addition to turning out tableware from about 1772 until after the close of the Revolution, he is known to have worked on the interior plaster decorations of dwellings constructed for miles around. He also found time to execute busts of persons prominent in that day.

The only contemporary sculpture of Washington is credited to Samuel Hill. It is a life-size bust portrait done in Jersey clay. Until a few years ago it adorned the pediment of a large window in the house built in 1775 for Daniel Hill, a brother of Samuel, on the Jersey side of the Delaware River near Washington's Crossing.

It is said that the bust was molded from an original carved in wood by Joseph Wright, an American sculptor, who lived in Bordentown between 1770 and 1790. The bust is of material similar to the hard-fired "stone" crocks produced at the Trenton and other Jersey potteries early in the nineteenth century from clay dug from pits near Perth Amboy. It is one of the best examples of native pottery and the earliest piece of such size thus far discovered. Its present whereabouts is unknown.

In 1805 Abraham Fulper established the Fulper Pottery Company at Flemington and that concern continues in existence. Its early products were stoneware, crocks, flowerpots, and glazed brown ware.

As early as 1779 Philip Durrell was conducting a pottery in Elizabethtown. The works were soon owned by Robert Hunt and were offered by him for sale on October 24, 1780,

Examples of New Jersey stoneware

in the *New Jersey Journal*. There appears to be no sale
recorded, or further mention of the venture until May 14,
1783, when Ichabod Halsey advertised that he had "erected
an earthenware factory in the town known as the Elizabethtown Earthen Manufactury." He appears to have continued
until 1790, in which year he advertised removal of his place
of business to the adjoining structure. On July 26, 1797, it
was offered for sale by John Durrell and by September 5,
1797, it had been sold to Willis & Steel, who operated it
until after 1800.

The second pottery to be set up in Elizbethtown is believed to have begun operations around 1816, and probably
was a rebirth of the one started by Durrell. Its owners
until 1835 are not known, but in that year a Mr. Pruden
was making yellow and Rockingham ware in addition to
stoneware. He continued until 1879, after which the factory
was taken over by L. B. Beerbower & Company and later
the Standard Sanitary Pottery Company.

During Pruden's time the stoneware produced included a
wide-mouthed jar of heavy gray glaze and brown lining,
with handles. Around the shoulder there were two dark
blue lines for decoration. Another piece credited to Pruden
in his later years is a heavy water pitcher probably inspired
by the centennial celebration of 1876 in Philadelphia. The
body of several pitchers so far discovered is fluted above a
ribbed border and on either side is the American eagle and
shield. The top is rimmed with a border of stars and beneath the covered spout is a scroll pattern.

A Samuel Dunham, who was employed at the Pruden
works, is credited with making large quantities of the slip-
decorated ware so commonly associated with the Pennsylvania Dutch country. When the Beerbower concern took
over the pottery, an inventory showed that whole stacks of
slip-decorated pie plates, platters, bowls, and other utensils
were found in the storehouse. Whether any of the ware has
survived the times is impossible to say, because it was not
marked in those days and is hardly to be distinguished from

the product of the Pennsylvania potteries.

The term "slip" was given by potters to clay that had been reduced to the consistency of cream by the addition of water. This thin paste was applied to the article of redware to be decorated, *after* a preliminary firing. Usually a quill or stalk of straw was used in the process, which consisted of tracing various designs or figures with light clay on darker surfaces, or vice versa.

In general, "slip" decoration was accomplished by first fashioning a piece of ware either on a potter's wheel, in a mold, or by means of coil spring to make the piece revolve. After it had been allowed to dry and harden, the slip mixture would be poured from the vat or pail into a smaller receptacle and then through a hollow tube or straw as the decorator traced the inscription or design directly on the article. The fancy decorating of cakes in these times closely resembles the art of slip-cup decoration.

Although the slip work was for decoration, it was applied to articles of utility, such as pie plates and platters. Usually it was beaten or rubbed level into such pieces, while on the more highly ornate pieces it was raised above the whole surface. After either process the articles were set in the sun in summer, or on a stove in winter, because the potters thought warmth was required for the glaze as a final detail.

As a first step the liquid was prepared and applied either by means of a horsehair brush or dipping. It was made from powdered lead and finely ground clay added to water, with sometimes a dye to give color other than the usual buff or yellow. The most common form of slip-decorated ware in New Jersey, however, was made of red clay with inscriptions or designs in yellow.

After the decoration was applied the articles were set to dry completely and then they were placed in a kiln for a week or more of firing. The process not only baked the clay hard, but it fused the glaze to its surface.

A pioneer potter in Trenton was John S. McCully, who in 1779 began to make pie plates and flower pots of red clay. Until 1852 he was without competitors, but in that year James Taylor, an Englishman, and Henry Speeler, a German, began the manufacture of yellow ware. They were followed in 1859 by Millington & Astbury and Rhodes & Yates, both of which concerns made white ware.

The Millington & Astbury firm produced the so-called Ellsworth pitcher of white pottery. It represents the shooting of Colonel Ellsworth at Alexandria, Virginia, at the outbreak of the Civil War, and the decorations were painted by Edward Lycett from designs by Josiah Janes. They were raised figures in color showing three men with the names Colonel Ellsworth, E. E. Brownell, and J. W. Jackson underneath. Such pitchers are marked "M. A. P., Trenton." The last letter was for a Poulson, who was taken in as a partner.

Other concerns started in that city a little later were Bloor, Ott & Booth, and William Youngs & Son. By 1863 there were ten potteries in Trenton and it had become the center of that industry. In 1873 the firm of Young, Astbury & Maddock, the latter a young Englishman, was started and marked the beginning of the development of fine china and pottery in this country. For many years, beginning about 1864, the East Trenton Pottery Works, founded by James Taylor, turned out earthen and enamel ware and is said to have been the first to produce hand-painted china.

The merger in 1892 of five successful and prominent Trenton firms into a single corporation is the answer to questions asked by numerous collectors seeking to know why the marks of certain New Jersey potteries cannot be found on pieces dating less than seventy-odd years ago.

The potteries were known as the Crescent, Delaware, Empire, Enterprise, and Equitable. They were brought under one management and operated as the Trenton Potteries Company. Previously they had been active in the city's life for various periods. In the case of Empire it was from 1863. Pieces of earthenware and china bearing their marks are eagerly sought.

The merger brought together the skilled employees, the formulas, and the managements of five separate enterprises. The combination afforded greater economies of manufacture through bulk production and the coordinate efforts of many expert potters.

The merged firm began experimenting in the manufacture of so-called solid porcelain products. It meant entering direct competition with foreign porcelain, which was being imported in large volume at the time. Pressure was brought to bear even to extend tariff protection to overcome the wage differential abroad.

At the time of consolidation, four of the potteries were turning out various objects of vitrified china, while the other ones manufactured tableware. The new plant became known as the Ideal Pottery and was the first in the country to produce porcelain bathtubs. Eventually manufacture was limited to all-clay plumbing fixtures for bathroom and kitchen.

The Empire Pottery Company was oldest of the merged firms. Organized in the midst of the Civil War period, it made during a thirty-year stretch many articles of earthenware and china that are now collector items. Its favorite mark was the word "Empire" over initials bordered by an acanthus leaf at either side and the address underneath. Later another mark used was in the form of a shield crossed at the middle with the word "Warrented" surmounted by a crown. "Imperial" was arched at the top of the shield and the single word "China" underneath.

The Enterprise Pottery Company was formed in Trenton in 1880, the Crescent Pottery in 1881, Delaware Pottery in 1884, and the Equitable Pottery in 1886. The only known mark used by Enterprise was its name without address. Crescent had two marks, the first a legend "Ironside China" underneath the figure of a king flanked by two maidens and the second a circle within a circle. Inside the smaller circle was the word "Utopia" over the word "Crescent." The entire second mark was above an oblong block within which there appeared "RO. No. 700."

Delaware Pottery used its name on the first of two marks with "Warrented" across the middle. The second mark omitted any word as identity. Equitable Pottery was the favorite name used by that firm, with occasionally a second mark consisting of an anchor under the word "Equitable" and over "Ironside."

Until about 1865 the products of Trenton potteries consisted almost entirely of heavy yellow and white earthenware and white granite ware of general similarity in shape and quality. For that reason, pieces that are not marked are extremely difficult to identify unless there is the history of ownership for a guide.

After decorated ware came in about 1865 it was quickly adopted by different firms. The first white ware to be decorated was produced at the Glasgow Pottery, founded in 1863 by John Moses & Company. The decoration consisted wholly of bands and lines of color and gold, and the work is said to have been done outside the potteries until after 1880. The initials "J. M. & S." were used on some of the tableware in the 1870s and 1880s, and also "Chios, Ironside."

The Mayer Pottery Company of Trenton was one of the six firms in the entire country to produce American majolica ware in the 1880-90s. Pieces remaining from its vast output of less than a century ago are uncommon enough today to be considered as scarce.

Imports of English-made majolica flooded the American market for a century before Mayer and his contemporaries started production. At its peak the Mayer pottery employed several hundred workers, including many brought over from England. Its ware was marked with the full name in a circle outside the word "Majolica."

The patterns of Mayer's majolica consisted of ferns, fruits, flowers, vegetables such as corn and cabbage, birds, fish, and animals. They were in raised designs, covered between firings by brilliant greens, reds, browns, and yellow beneath a glazed finish. Other pieces worth collecting are in the shape of fans, shells, owls, parrots, swans, and ducks.

High on the roll of American potters is the name of Walter Lenox, founder of the Lenox Potteries, which has come to be known the world over for its rare and beautiful products. Lenox was born in Trenton in 1859. As a boy he early showed an interest in the potteries, where dull lumps of clay were made into dishes and vessels by the rapid spinning of the potter's wheel.

As a young man Lenox became apprenticed in the potter's craft and his spare hours were devoted to experimenting with design and color. He soon became art director of the Ott & Brewer factory, at the time an important concern in Trenton. He was ever on the alert to improve the quality of products and eventually succeeded in raising money to start a pottery of his own.

Just as Lenox was about to realize his ambition to produce a creamy, richly glazed china, he was stricken with paralysis and blindness in 1895. With the help of faithful aides he continued to strive for perfection and never abandoned the goal during many years of adversity.

Lenox died in 1920, but his principles have carried the potteries he founded to leadership among makers of fine china. The Lenox mark is known all over the world and appears on seventeen hundred pieces in the White House dinner service and on other sets renowned for their art. With all the advance of modern industry, the skill of the individual craftsman continues to be the secret of success in Lenox potteries.

In 1854 the American Porcelain Manufacturing Co. was formed at Gloucester in South Jersey. It was both a financial and commercial failure and was followed in 1857 by the Gloucester China Company. The quality of its porcelain ware was good, but the workmanship was poor. There was no attempt at decoration and all pieces were sold in the white "except for such ornamentation or relief as might be produced by the moulds." The glazing and firing were of inferior grade and the ware was marketed in a blistered and rough condition. It is said that large quantities of imperfect pieces were dumped along the river bank near the pottery and the place came to be known as "China Wharf" before production stopped about 1860.

Early records of a pottery in Rahway tell of a venture started in 1830 by John Mann for the production of earthenware. All trace of its location and other details has been lost. Two years earlier John Hancock, who had served an apprenticeship with Josiah Wedgewood in England, started a works in South Amboy for stone and yellow ware.

A pottery was established at Haddonfield as early as 1805. Among the various owners were Charles Wingender & Brother and Richard Snowden. In 1880 the products were stoneware mugs, tankards, and water coolers.

Although there undoubtedly were individuals who worked the clays of that region at an earlier date, the first firm of potters recorded near South Amboy was Warne & Letts, which produced stoneware beginning around 1806. Later William Hancock, an Englishman, established a place on the beach at the foot of the Bordentown Turnpike, and it became known as the Congress Hill Pottery, where a good-quality white china was made.

After several years Hancock was succeeded by George Price, who with others carried on the manufacture of stoneware. For a time prior to 1849 the wooden building, resting on a brick foundation, was idle. In that year Abraham Cadmus began the production of yellow and Rockingham ware and continued in the business until his death in 1854. It was reopened in 1857 by Joseph Wooton, passed to William A. Allen in 1860, and the following year was destroyed by fire.

One of the articles produced during the proprietorship of Cadmus was a mug-shaped pitcher, with a bright glaze and the spout just below the rim. It was decorated with raised grape leaves, and a rustic handle was forked at the top, where it fastened on the body.

With the end of the Civil War, pottery and earthenware

manufactures were set up in South Amboy. One of the first was the Swan Hill Pottery, the proprietors of which were James Carr, Thomas Locker, and Joseph Watson. From old billheads dated 1870 it is known that the concern advertised white ware, yellow ware, enameled ware, and Rockingham ware. Later James Carr & Co. conducted a similar business. Other South Amboy potters of the 1870s were James L. Rue & Co., operating as successors to James Wiseman & Co., and Charles Fish & Co. These concerns produced Rockingham and yellow ware.

The Eagle Pottery, dating from about 1858, was one of the early Perth Amboy enterprises, although the factory was situated on the road to Woodbridge. Its first proprietor was William Benton and the superintendent was George Barlow, an Englishman. Most of the workmen were from Staffordshire, in England. Prior to merger with a fire brick concern in 1865, they produced fine-quality brown glazed and yellow earthenware.

One of the Eagle Pottery items was a creamer, although pitchers, jugs, bowls, and other articles were made. It is said that the yellow ware was exceptionally popular just before the outbreak of the Civil War.

About 1840 a Captain Thomas Gould owned a flourishing pottery in Caldwell, on what was then called the Center Hill Road. He made stoneware crocks of gray glaze and black lining, wide mouth, and handles, without decoration.

At Lambertville, in 1848, Joseph Raisner had a pottery where he made red earthenware for household use. The products included milk pans, colanders, pie plates, and jugs. He also turned out money jugs in the form of vases without handles. They had a knob on top and a slot at the side for coins. His wares were not marked, but a variety of articles have been identified as coming from the old factory in Hancock Street and include a red earthenware jug with lustrous black glaze, specked with metallic spots. The pie plates that have been found have indented edges and yellow splashed on the reddish surface.

Trace has been found of several potteries in the vicinity of Hackensack beginning around 1815, but they appear to have been devoted to the making of brick. At Little Ferry there were clay banks where material was obtained for Newark potteries.

Prior to 1810 Captain Ephraim MacKay was conducting a pottery at New Brunswick. In that year he offered "his residence and exclusive pot house for sale," but in 1822 he advised his fellow townsmen that he had enlarged "that portion of the factory lately destroyed by fire," from which it may be taken that he had continued in business. As a matter of fact it is known that, until shortly before his death in 1826, he produced an assortment of tiles and earthenware, as well as black teapots similar to the one that is illustrated.

The MacKay works continued until about 1880. Among those connected with it after the founder's death were A. J. Butler and Adam Green.

Another New Brunswick pottery was located in Water Street about 1830. It was operated by Homer & Shirley, who made flint stoneware and small pitchers and mugs that were decorated with raised figures.

A few miles away at Woodbridge the Salamander Pottery was established in 1825 by Michael Lefoulon, and at one time it was the largest clay-products plant in the state. Lefoulon, who was lost at sea in 1842, was succeeded by Henry De Casse and in 1867 the owners were Poillon & Weidner. The concern had a steady growth until the factory, employing one hundred and twenty-five persons and having eight kilns at the time, was destroyed by fire in 1896.

After De Casse's time the Salamander works turned out mostly pipes, bricks, and other industrial products, but prior to 1860 Rockingham ware was made. Examples that have been positively identified include the Hound-Handled Pitchers in various sizes, which are distinguished by an indented border at the shoulder just above the hunting scene.

Early stoneware teapot

The Jersey City Pottery was the first such enterprise in that city. It was started prior to 1825 by two Frenchmen whose names are not known and they are credited with producing a white porcelain ware new to this country. It marked the start of an era in pottery making and led in that year to an act of the state Legislature creating the New Jersey Porcelain & Earthenware Company. The finances were supplied by George Dummer, Timothy Dewey, Henry Post, Jr., William N. Shirley and Robert Abbott, who were not potters. Their workmen, however, were so skilled that in 1826 a silver medal was won at the Franklin Institute in Philadelphia for the excellence of their white ware, represented now by a piece in the Turnbull collection at Princeton University.

The Jersey City concern produced common white and yellow earthenware, but during its somewhat brief success its specialty was the hard-paste porcelain of excellent body and glaze usually decorated with a gold stripe. This required transporting from the South supplies of china clay or kaolin, because New Jersey has always lacked such deposits in spite of the abundance of fire, stoneware, and other clays.

Porcelain is a ceramic term applied to many different kinds of ware, but all true porcelains must be made of white-burning, finely ground materials, including white china clay or kaolin for plasticity, feldspar, or petuntse for transparency, and pulverized silica or flint. True porcelain differs from other pottery because it is translucent.

While we are on the subject of distinctions in earthen-

Fruit bowl of stoneware

Earthenware oil lamp

ware, it may be well to describe the principal characteristics of the other products turned out by New Jersey potters and here discussed. White stoneware is so called because it is made from a clay that turns white when burned on account of having been mixed with flint. Rockingham ware is a variety of coarse earthenware made of a red or buff burning clay and covered with a brown glaze. It is so named after the Marquis of Rockingham, on whose estate it first was made.

One of the best-known examples of Rockingham ware in this country is a toby jug, made at the Jersey City Pottery after it had encountered financial difficulties in 1828 and failed. The pottery was purchased in that year by David Henderson and his brother, who carried on until 1833 as D & J Henderson. They produced the white stone china and Rockingham described, also a common yellow earthenware.

In 1833 the firm became the American Pottery Company; a few years later it adopted the English method of transfer printing in decoration when it was first introduced in this country. During the Presidential campaign of 1840 it turned out great numbers of cream-colored pitchers and mugs bearing the portrait of Harrison in black transfer print under the glaze. Those preserved are octagonal in shape and four panels have the Harrison picture. His name appears underneath and a log cabin above, while the legend "The Ohio Farmer" is beneath the figure of an American Eagle.

Early in the 1840s, Daniel Greatsback, an English potter, joined the Jersey City concern. He designed a large number of pieces, including an earthen water pitcher, decorated in relief with hunting scenes and a deerhound-shaped handle. By 1848 the pottery was turning out druggists' jars in blue and white trim after the style of pieces now preserved in the Pennsylvania Museum.

James O. Rouse and Nathaniel Turner came into ownership of the factory in 1850 and returned it to the name of the Jersey City Pottery. Their products were marked with a lion and a unicorn on either side of a shield, with the letters "R. & T." below. It was the first use of the British type of mark on American ware and soon other potters followed the practice in seeking to overcome the preference for foreign products.

Between 1837 and 1875 there were several potteries

operating in Newark. In the first-mentioned year Balthasar Krumeich owned a small factory in South Canal Street, where he made money jugs, preserve jars, cups, pie plates, and various kinds of yellow and brown ware. The establishment continued in the family for many years after his death.

Daniel Gillig had a pottery in Ogden Street, Newark, before he moved to Orange Street in 1855, when he took a partner by the name of Williams. Later, John H. Osborn succeeded the latter and the business was relocated in North Broad Street (now Belleville Avenue). In 1862 it was known as the Newark Pottery and it continued for years in the Osborn family. In the beginning stoneware and earthenware were produced, but eventually drainpipe and portable furnaces were manufactured, although yellow and Rockingham ware, probably obtained elsewhere, were advertised.

In 1854 Robert Atcheson, J. P. Atcheson, and Isaac Ogden founded the firm of Robert Atcheson & Company at Chestnut and McWhorter Streets, Newark, and in 1874 it was owned by Ogden. The output was much the same as at the Gillig & Osborn plant. Two years earlier Franz Haefeli and several others started the manufacture of terra-cotta ware, statuary, and house ornaments at Pacific and Nichols Streets, but the venture soon failed. Another firm was the Union Pottery, established in 1871 to make stoneware, earthenware, and other products in a factory at Bloomfield Avenue and the Morris Canal. After the business was taken over by Haidle & Zipt in 1875, one of the articles sold was a stoneware crock with vertical sides, heavy rim, a gray glazed exterior, and black lining. It had a floral design in dark blue and a handle.

The marks used by only a small portion of New Jersey potterers are definitely known. Undoubtedly many of them did not adopt a distinctive mark, while others copied those of English potters. The Thomas Maddock's Sons Company has traced the marks of a considerable number of Jersey producers. They are illustrated in the Appendix to this volume.

9

Iron, Brass, Copper, Tin, and Lead

*N*o account of New Jersey's craftsmen would be complete unless it included reference to the metal workers of colonial times. Almost simultaneously with the first permanent settlements, discovery was made of iron, copper, and other mineral resources. Thus it was natural that the material so close at hand would be utilized in fashioning necessities of life. For many years shipments of ore were made to the other colonies and abroad for the same purpose.

Little is known by name of Jersey's early metal craftsmen, but there is abundant evidence of their skill. It is next to impossible to identify them, because the numerous articles they made were not such as to prompt marking, nor was production limited to a few individuals. Many of the quaintly fashioned pieces brought to light in recent years through a growing appreciation of their worth show every indication of genuine ability; others undoubtedly were the result of a chance hand to meet necessity.

By far the most important metal was iron. A great deal of it was deposited in the northeast portion of the state and "bog-iron" was found in the southern region. The first iron works are said to have been built near Shrewsbury about 1674 and from then on others were set up over a wide area. Gradually the iron forges and furnaces came

under control of what were in those days powerful interests, and during the Revolution they were important for
the supplies furnished to the Continental forces.

The early forges and furnaces were located on streams
and near forests, like the glass houses. They were worked
largely by indentured labor from England, Ireland, and
Germany, and, particularly in the northern section, by slaves.

Some of the forges where bar iron was made directly
from the ore were much like the blacksmith's forge, except
that they were wider and deeper. Others used pig iron
made from bar iron and there had to be furnaces to melt
the ore and stamping mills to crush the hardened mass,
usually with a heavy iron drop hammer operated by a water
wheel.

Furnaces were required to reduce both bog and hard iron
ore to metallic iron. They usually consisted of a four-sided
stack of stone or brick, about twenty feet high and from
twenty to twenty-four feet square at the base. Inside, separated by a lining of sand or broken stone, was a center core
open at both ends and usually made of fire bricks. It was
perhaps ten feet square at the base and tapered to eight
feet over a hearth on which the fire was made to heat the
interior of the furnace.

The ore filled the space between the core and outer walls;
as it melted, impurities rose to the top to be drawn off. In
nine or ten hours the molten iron was allowed to run off at
an opening at the bottom into sand gutters and then into
crude oblong molds.

At first the lining of a furnace lasted only sixteen to
eighteen weeks, but later better methods of construction
increased the time to from six to eight months. The ore was
fed in at the top and the fires kept constantly at top heat.
Usually the forges could run all year, but furnaces with air
blasts could operate by water wheel only so long as the
weather was not freezing.

The forges and furnaces of New Jersey are a story in
themselves and it would not be possible here to tell of them

Iron chest from Sterling Foundry

all, or of the men identified with the various enterprises. Although the community smiths turned out a great deal of the iron work in which we are interested today, most of the producers of iron took a hand at it and were responsible for the first stoves, firebacks, and heavier articles, as well as utensils of many kinds.

Bars bearing the imprint of various furnaces have been found, but for the most part it is possible to identify only firebacks as to origin, because they were either marked or of a design attributed to a particular forge. For instance, the Aetna Furnace in Cumberland County turned out a fireback depicting a deer, and the name of the Cumberland Furnace showed in raised lettering across the top. Those made at the Oxford Furnace showed lions on hind legs holding aloft a crown, or the figures of a maid and man holding hands.

FIRE BACK FROM ÆTNA FURNACE

Aetna furnace fire back

The *New York Gazette* and *Weekly Mercury* for March 12, 1770, printed this advertisement of the Vesuvius Furnace:

> Vesuvius Furnace—Wanted immediately. At Vesuvius Furnace, at Newark, East New Jersey, two persons who understand molding of Hollow Ware in Sand.

In the *New Jersey Journal* of October 24, 1781, there appeared an advertisement that gives an idea of the role played by the early forges and furnaces. It read:

> To be sold or exchanged for country produce and other articles necessary to carry on an iron works, etc.: All sorts of cast iron kettles, pots, large and small tea kettles, pie pans, large and small skillets, small mortars, griddles with and without legs; wagon chair and cart boxes, close stoves, six and ten plate stoves, open fire places, commonly called 'Franklin stoves' etc., etc., etc.,— wholesale and retail by the subscriber at Morris Co. Furnace— John Jacob Faesch.

Faesch was one of the leading iron manufacturers of his day. Probably a Swiss, he came to this country in 1765 and after working for a time at the Ringwood forge, with a brief period as manager, he established himself at Mount Hope. His house remains standing in that town, where he reigned for years as a leading citizen. During the Revolution, Washington visited him there and as one result Faesch obtained permission to work Hessian prisoners in the nearby mines.

Stove plates and firebacks were among the early products of cast iron, and they began to be made in New Jersey during the middle of the eighteenth century. Most of the fragments discovered today are parts from the old five-plate and six-plate stoves popular in that period. Although primitive in design, they had a wide range of shapes. Approximately two feet square, they were clamped together in the form of a box to be set into a chimney jamb or the back of a fireplace. Glowing embers were shoveled into the box and allowed to smolder. The heat was thrown off from

Plate from Cumberland furnace

the front and also the rear, where the stove projected into an adjoining room.

The top and bottom plates of these old "jamb stoves" were plain, while the two side plates and the end plates were ornamented at the time of casting with various figures and designs. Sometimes the five-plate stove had two legs on

Dutch oven door

the side farthest from the wall, while the six-plate stove, which came a little later, projected into the room, with a stovepipe, fuel door, and an opening to give off heat.

Casting of stove plates was done in open sand and the molds were of wood or clay. The patterns were executed to represent incidents of biblical or legendary significance. On occasion they bore quaint sayings or verses, and many of them were inscribed with the date they were made. The best period of design for the cast-iron stove plates was from 1740 to 1760. After that the "ten-plate" stove came into use and evidence of individuality and skill gradually gave way to plainness.

Two of the six-plate stoves made at the Atsion Furnace in Burlington County are in the First Presbyterian Church at Bridgeton. They apparently date about 1815 and have a hearth extension on the bottom plate. Another Atsion

stove is still in service in the Chesterfield Meeting House in
Burlington County.

It is unusual to find complete stoves as they were made
at the old Jersey furnaces, but various parts may be located
in out-of-the-way places. The front plates are eagerly sought
by collectors because of the various designs and identifying
marks that tie them up with one of the state's earliest
industries.

Stoves made in New Jersey when the furnaces were at a
peak were shipped by boat up the Hudson River and along
the Atlantic coast. They helped to heat homes and churches
in many parts of the country from 1750 on.

The first Franklin stoves were made at the forge of
Martin Ryerson at Pompton in Passaic County and they
found a ready sale among the Dutch inhabitants in and
around Bergen. Coal was used in them first around 1826,
and afterward in open grates.

In New Jersey, as in the other colonies, the blacksmith
was a personage of importance during the early days and
nearly every community had at least one member of the
craft. He shod the horses, mended the wagons, and performed numerous other services for his neighbors. In addition he wrought on his anvil iron hinges of all kinds and
designs, latches, knockers, handles, keys, gates, railings,
foot-scrapers, weather vanes, and bolts, among a score of
articles.

Here and there over the countryside an ancient house
may be found with some of the original hardware remaining, but for the most part it has disappeared with the passing
of years. More often reproductions of the old pieces will
be seen, but there will not be the same attraction, or evidence of individuality.

The Dutch houses of northern New Jersey were splen-
didly adapted to the decorative ironwork turned out by
smithies of the region. On most of them doors and window
shutters were hung with strap hinges extending across the
entire width. At the large end they were bent to fit over a

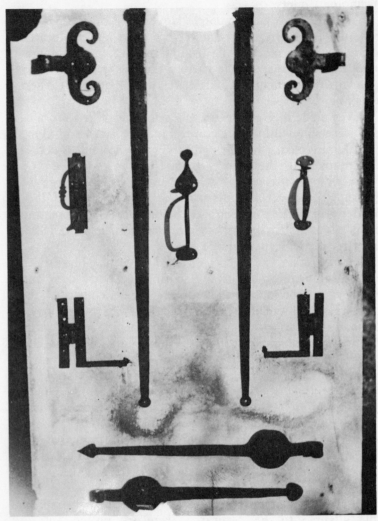

Wrought iron hinges and latches

pin fastened into the frame, with turned out ends above
and below. The hinges were a single piece of metal, tapering
to a small end that nearly always was ornamented.

The strap hinges on north Jersey houses were distinguished by the form of a circle near the eye end. In other
parts of the state where the Dutch influence was not so
strong the small end of the hinges was spear shaped. The
H and T hinges, so called because they were fashioned like
those letters, also were popular. The angle hinge was a
fourth type.

Another feature of the Dutch houses was the combination
handle and knocker found on many of the divided doors.
Elsewhere they were usually separate and followed one of
several different types, with minor variations according to
the whims of the maker. Latches, grasps, and knobs were
confined to a few styles, but they differed in size and ornamentation.

On the more pretentious dwellings it was a sign of standing in the community to have a nameplate on the door and
these devices offered splendid opportunity for decorative
skill. The same was true of keyplates. The heads of keys
were made in a variety of shapes, but the key stems, locks,
and bolts were massive and difficult to make in other than
simple design. Door knockers of iron are scarce, because
they came before those of brass and were not made in great
number. They were, however, well done, in both heavy and
gracefully light style in a variety of designs.

Foot scrapers for front doorsteps, weather vanes atop
the ridge pole of barns, and tie-irons used to support heavy
timbers were other objects of the blacksmith's skill. They
were turned out in such varied shapes and designs that to
attempt description might result in leaving out some of the
best.

In gates and railings the blacksmith had his best opportunity to utilize decoration. Excellent examples of both cast
and wrought iron work of that sort still are to be found
where older houses remain in Elizabeth, Newark, Morris-

town, and other cities about the state dating from colonial days.

Iron work fashioned by the early smithies to serve as railings for stairways and to enclose front yards has served as inspiration for reproduction to this day. The same is true of balcony guards and the grille work used to protect first-floor windows and decorate front porches.

Many articles made from iron were used around the fireplace and served purposes essential to life in the home. Early andirons were fashioned in countless designs and shapes, with the feet, stocks, and finials offering splendid opportunity for display of the smith's skill. They were made to represent animals or serpents. Early in the nineteenth century they were decorated with figures cast in brass, with the American eagle and seal of the United States forming favorite designs.

Eighteenth-century fireplace equipment

Early New Jersey lighting devices. COURTESY RICHARD C. GAINE

Tongs and the handles of hearth shovels usually were decorated, and it was quite the style to make them harmonize with the andirons. Across the front of parlor and bedroom fireplaces were placed scrolled bars or low grille work to keep members of the family from getting too close to the fire and prevent the hot embers from setting fire to wooden floors.

Trivets and kettle arms of graceful proportion were common to many fireplaces and added to the fireside charm besides serving a utilitarian purpose.

Cooking utensils, as a rule, were plain in design, or only the handles were ornamented. Waffle irons were an exception, fashioned in a variety of designs. The exteriors frequently bore scroll work or floral figures, and the inner surfaces were so cast that the waffles were baked with impressions calculated to give added pleasure to eating.

Early lanterns and lamps were made of iron. There were the graceful hanging creations with open sides to throw off the oil or candle light. The oldest types were sometimes fitted with oiled paper; later, glass was utilized. Little whale and lard oil lamps and the so-called "Betty" lamps, which were hung on the backs of chairs or near the mantel piece, were popular.

The casting of brass seems not to have been undertaken in this country until around 1800. Previously most articles of brass had come from England and only a limited quantity of the alloy had been available by importation. As a matter of fact, England encouraged the exportation of raw materials to the colonies, and did little to promote their industry.

When brass did come into use, the smiths of New Jersey were among the first to sense its decorative possibilities, and in time it replaced iron for the making of many articles. They included andirons and other hearth-place paraphernalia, door knockers and knobs, candlesticks, and warming-pan lids. Brass buttons also were in popular demand, although they had been made many years before in Philadelphia by Casper Wistar, who obtained therefrom the money with which to set up his glass-blowing venture in South Jersey. The brass he used was obtained from England.

Many of the brass articles attributed to early American make probably originated in England. The styles were very similar and the workmanship every bit as good. With the advent of American brass came a tendency to elaborate in style, but it did not lead to any inventive turn or development of other changes.

Copper, although one of the mineral products of New Jersey, was not used extensively during the colonial period. Some kettles were made of the metal, but the difficulty of cleaning did not appeal to the women folk. Partly on account of the contrast of color, figures and designs were cut frequently from copper to decorate tin and lead articles such as warming pans and sconces.

Tin alloy was turned to various uses and to some extent was a substitute when pewter could not be so readily obtained. It was more easily worked and when kept from the effects of damp weather by a coat of paint would not rust. On the other hand, articles of tin could be burnished almost to the brilliancy of silver and were not nearly so costly.

There is no record by name of old tinsmiths in New Jersey. Undoubtedly there were some. It is probable, too, that the early blacksmiths worked in tin when occasion demanded. In the middle nineteenth century tinsmiths from Connecticut and Pennsylvania peddled their wares throughout the state, hence it is virtually impossible to fix the origin of a particular article.

Teapots, cups, trays, candleboxes, candlesticks, candle molds, sconces, lanthorns, sand shakers, foot warmers, and hand warmers were among the articles of household utility made from tin alloy. Some of those pieces offered splendid opportunity for decoration, which was accomplished either by hammering to produce an embossed effect or by punching. Engraved or scratched designs were other forms of decoration; painting, or japanning, was a separate art.

Hammering or punching as a means of decoration was most common on sconces, which were fastened against the wall. They were of various shapes and frequently copper silhouettes were added to them. Candle molds usually were plain and were of different sizes, while candle boxes and candlesticks tended toward the decorative. The boxes, often round and worked in perforated or punched effects, were to be found in a handy place in almost every kitchen.

The perforated or punched design showed at its best in the lanthorns, or candle lanterns. Cylindrical or square in shape, and with a ring handle to hold them by, they threw off light in proportion to the number of holes, usually worked into ornamental patterns. Lanthorns lighted the way to church for Jersey villagers on dark Sunday evenings and were hung over doorways.

Foot and hand warmers were other articles where perforation was a necessity. Filled with hot coals, they gave some comfort against the cold during lengthy church services and on wintery rides. The holes were punched in different designs to let off the heat and some warmers fitted into wooden frames with handles.

Mention has been made of engraved or scratched designs on tin articles. Examples of such work may be found on the old pitchers, cups, and trays, but painting was even more highly favored. In the succeeding chapter that form of decorative hand art will be explained more in detail.

Lead was employed only to a minor extent by Jersey craftsmen. Occasionally it was used in casting cornice designs, urns, and other exterior decoration. Headboxes of water drains and the old-time fire plaques adopted by insurance companies were also made of lead.

It is fairly certain that very few, if any, articles of lead antedate the Revolution, insofar as New Jersey is concerned. During the struggle everything of that metal was taken for bullets. Doubtless many of the early fire marks first adopted by the Mutual Assurance Company of Philadelphia, which was organized in 1752, met such an end. They were the most interesting articles of lead and were fastened on the outside of houses and other buildings as an indication that there was insurance. A double purpose was served, because volunteer bucket brigades thus knew that they would be rewarded for extinguishing a fire, and enemies of persons owning structures so marked were less apt to seek vengeance by resort to arson.

It is not known that fire marks were made in New Jersey, although in the early days of insurance many of them were affixed to dwellings in the western part of the state. The insurance was carried mostly in Philadelphia companies and these emblems probably originated in that city. A pine tree was the sign adopted by one company, clasped hands in various positions was a favorite insignia, and a replica of a hose cart was another.

Leaden firemarks

Decorative Painting and Carving

*D*ecorative painting and carving were of considerable
importance in New Jersey's colonial and post-
colonial periods. They served to satisfy individual desires
for ornamentation of numerous articles of household utility
and for recording historical events in a manner more vivid
than could be accomplished by the written word.

Both forms of handiwork came to this country from the
Old World, and to the Dutch must be given first credit for
their use. Of course, the English also possessed the urge for
embellishing their things, but they practiced more restraint.
It is in the northern part of the state and the Raritan River
valley region where examples of early decorative effort are
found at the best.

At first decorative painting was almost entirely a matter
of amateur effort. By that I mean that the colonists made
use of colors to brighten, as best they could, the articles
at hand. The habit never entirely ended, as is manifested
by the numbers of chairs, tables, and chests with several
layers of paint that every collector has discovered. Eventually cabinetmakers and other craftsmen sought to add to the
attractiveness of their work and the itinerant decorator
came into demand.

There are abundant examples of decorative painting
undeniably of New Jersey origin. In addition to the furni-

Painted metal tray

ture already mentioned there are clock dials and doors, framed mirror tops, trays and other pieces of tin and wooden ware, boxes of various sizes and designs, bellows, shop and tavern signs, and a miscellany of small objects.

A great deal of the early furniture made in New Jersey was of pine and other native woods that were easily worked. Much of it was plain in design and line, and paint was easy to apply to brighten up surroundings. In addition, it was a wood preservative, which undoubtedly is one reason why Jerseymen were so given to the use of the familiar red and blue colors. In New Jersey, more than in the other colonies, furniture was covered entirely with paint, but many examples are to be found where it was applied to only a part of the surface in decorative design.

The kas, or Dutch cupboard, afforded an opportunity for decorative painting. The first of such huge pieces were brought from Holland, and several splendid examples from across the sea are known to be cherished possessions of families in the Raritan River valley region. Many were made of walnut, but more often there was a combination of woods. On the last-mentioned, flowers, fruit, and ribbons were painted on the side panels and face of the doors.

Corner cupboards also were painted, but designs were seldom attempted. Usually of pine, the entire exterior was covered with a blue or white, with the inside done in a contrasting color. Sometimes the arch forming the top was decorated, although more often it was either left plain or embellished with a bit of carving.

The painted chairs and benches, or settees, of Jersey origin appear to have come mostly from Monmouth County, which was the early center for chairmaking in this state. On the rush-bottom chairs, after the entire surface had been covered with black or white paint, garlands of flowers or other designs were run across the topmost splat and on the short apron piece around the seat. There was ample room on the benches used both indoors and on front porches to make decorative designs.

Decorative painting for chairs, as distinguished from the use of solid color, became most popular toward the end of the eighteenth and first part of the nineteenth centuries. Green, yellow, brown, gray, and black had been added by that time to the red and blue of earlier days. White was generally reserved for the chairs for the best front room.

The first painted designs of lines and bands were applied free hand. Then a transfer method was adopted, somewhat like the application of decalcomanias, and it was possible to achieve more elaborate effects. Finally, the American Empire period of the early 1800s saw the advent of the stencil and also the use of gilt. Designs were stenciled not only in color, but gilt was favored as a sort of substitute for brass mounts on chairs and some other articles of more cheaply made furniture. It even, to some extent, replaced the inlay, which required more work and skill.

Some examples of decorative painting, particularly on chairs, are to be found in an excellent condition. Occasionally the removal of a layer of paint applied at a later date will bring to light such handiwork, usually capable of very acceptable restoration. There are several Jersey craftsmen of the present day who have acquired the knack of applying designs in the old ways, and they have returned many a piece to its former glory.

Clocks offered another opportunity for the use of paint. It was seldom put on the cases, although sometimes carved flowers near the pediment were colored. The dials were the principal objects of embellishment and they afforded the excuse for a variety of designs. Jolly-looking round-faced moons were common on the dials of nearly all eight-day tall clocks with astronomical attachments, and usually they shone out from skies studded with stars. Occasionally square-rigged ships floated majestically on wavy seas.

In the lower corners of the dials it was the custom to paint in floral designs, baskets of fruit, birds in gay colors, or other effects. The clockmakers seldom attempted to make their own dials. They were purchased, and occasionally the initials or name of the individual who painted them will be found, although usually the name of the clockmaker was inscribed across the face.

The dials of clocks without the astronomical movement seemed to invite more varied efforts. Birds and fruits were painted most frequently and with varying degrees of success, ranging from evidence of real skill to crude likenesses. Now and then a religious subject was adopted. The dials were either of metal or wood.

Paintings on glass constituted another decorative effort among Jersey craftsmen, from the late eighteenth century onward. Found principally on the panel head of mirrors and the doors of shelf and wall clocks, they are seldom signed, or at best show only initials. That is undoubtedly one reason why no painters native to New Jersey have been

Painting on glass

identified, but the choice of local scenes for such work has established their existence.

Mirrors with a painted panel were almost always enclosed in a frame of mahogany or native wood, which was stained or varnished. The views ranged from bits of countryside that might be found in sections of Monmouth County or the rolling Somerset hills to Washington's Headquarters at Morristown or the Battle of Trenton. The colors were limited, usually to bright greens, reds, or blues, and to white, which were thickly and often poorly applied. Washington and other Revolutionary heroes also were depicted, on the American flag, with festoons of laurel for decoration.

The painting of mirrors was copied from England and France. They were imported by the wealthier people and those of foreign origin may be picked out because of the better quality of the painting. Then, too, the native glass was not so expertly silvered and with the passing of years the reflecting surface has become clouded.

Comparatively few clocks of the shelf or wall type were made in New Jersey. Most of those found in the state came from Connecticut and were brought here on peddlers' carts. They date from the early years of the nineteenth century and the painted doors are on the whole better done. Usually the doors were divided into two panels, with the upper part over the dial of clear glass and the lower half covered by a painting executed on the reverse side. Birds were favorite subjects on the shelf-type clocks, while military scenes, country landscapes, and a front view of Mount Vernon appeared most frequently on the hanging or banjo clocks.

Trays of wood and tin in various sizes, and oval, round, or oblong in shape, were common in New Jersey homes from shortly after the eighteenth century. They were covered first with a coat of black paint and designs of fruits and flowers, with sometimes birds or bits of landscape worked on in colors. Nearly always there was a wide border of gilt scroll over the rolled edges. A coat of lacquer or thin varnish was applied over the whole top surface for preservation.

Tea and coffee pots, canisters, and other small tin articles of household utility were embellished with painted floral designs. Boxes of all sizes and for a variety of uses were treated similarly, and lamps placed over doorways were covered with a coat of black paint as protection against the weather.

There was some decorative painting on leather in New Jersey's post-colonial years. Tanned hides were quite often used to cover small trunks or chests, and the urge for embellishment now and then led to the tracing of an owner's name on the top, surrounded by floral designs. Frequently these served as hope chests for prospective brides and have been found years after stored carefully under attic eaves as containers of momentoes that went back to courtship days.

Leather buckets and hats of early volunteer fire brigades were decorated with designs and figures symbolic of the names by which they were known. The eagle and American shield were two favorites. Such relics are hard to find nowadays and, for the most part, are in the possession of fire companies whose existence dates from one of the pioneer organizations, or are jealously guarded by descendants of members.

Painted and carved sign-boards and figures are certainly worthy of mention in any account of decorative handiwork in New Jersey. Here again it is almost impossible to identify the craftsmen who were responsible for them. Some, doubtless, were native to this region, but others were itinerants who roamed the countryside, with here and there an individual whose skill made him deserving of an artist's ranking.

In any event, signs were useful as well as colorful adjuncts to daily life in the eighteenth and nineteenth centuries. Prior to the time when there were named streets with numbered houses and when comparatively few people could read, they were sought by men of all trades and innkeepers, especially, to attract customers or the weary traveler.

Signboards and figures were familiar in all of the colonies, but nowhere were they more numerous and more picturesque than in New Jersey. As education progressed, newspapers increased in numbers and circulation, thoroughfares were designated by names, and the use of business signs dwindled. They lingered sometimes because they were the guarantee of an established concern, but today it is exceedingly difficult to locate such a sign of authenticated origin.

Old histories of New Brunswick, when it was one of the thriving seaports along the Atlantic Coast, describe the scene along its busy riverfront. There were the drygoods merchants, naval stores purveyors, grain and cattle dealers, and a score of others. Each one invited patronage by displaying at the front of his shop a sign, designed by quaintness, appropriateness, or costliness to attract customers and fix in their memories the exact location of the advertiser.

In Newark, Elizabeth, Morristown, and a dozen other towns, signs were familiar in the old days. The clockmaker, goldsmith, hatter, and all the other tradesmen made use of them. The legends and objects painted on some of the signs were appropriate enough. The saddlemaker was identified by a saddle or horse, the bootmaker by a boot, the hatter by a hat, and so on. Other signs were without significance, either in relation to the business they indicated or in the association of the objects to which they referred. Usually, however, they were qualified to accomplish their purpose, suspended over shop doorways as objects of attraction to the public.

The tavern sign often was only a board painted legibly with a name, but many times it was an elaborate emblem. It was attached to a wooden or wrought-iron arm fashioned like a fire crane, projecting from the structure or a post. Occasionally it was hung from a substantial frame erected in front of the establishment, and in such cases one of the poles was quite likely to support a weather vane.

Taverns were familiar to every hamlet and town in New Jersey. Around them community life centered and, in addition, they were stopping places for man and beast in the old stagecoach days. Prior to the Revolution they were known by names brought from the Old World or those having neighborhood significance. There was the Red Lion Inn, King George's Inn, The Wheat Sheaf Inn, and The Three Crowns Inn, to name only a few.

When war clouds began to thicken, the taverns became gathering places for patriots who planned resistance to English rule. When the conflict broke out and armed forces fought back and forth over Jersey soil, those same taverns gave lodging to Washington and many other Revolutionary heroes. The old Arnold Tavern in Morristown, where Alexander Hamilton first met Betty Schuyler, was one such place.

The struggle for independence led to a postwar change in the names of many taverns and roadhouses. Those whose owners could lay the slightest claim to the honor were called "The Washington House" as an indication that the nation's first citizen had stopped there. Others were known as The Lafayette House, or by some equally patriotic name.

The variety of tavern signs was as wide as the number of such establishments. Even those which bore the same name were identified by different signs. Washington was pictured in one instance by just the head and shoulders, in another astride a horse, and again standing under a tree. Lafayette and other Revolutionary heroes were shown in the same poses, and a sheaf of wheat, trees, and animals also were used.

It is extremely doubtful if any of the original signboards have survived the passing of time. Exposure to the weather did not make for long existence and the wood quite likely split or rotted eventually, even though repainting frequently was undertaken as a precaution. In some instances the signs

Jersey tavern sign

still to be found here and there over the state that mark some of the old inns may well be faithful replicas of those earlier ones. Even so, there is a story and something fascinating in searching for them.

Hand painting of chinaware should be mentioned among the pioneer decorative arts of New Jersey, even though it originated around 1865. At first only bands and lines of color and gold were used, but in a short time birds and floral designs were the style and scenes of historic events became popular. The hand decorating of china really was a step beyond the so-called slip method of ornamenting pottery and earthenware that had been practiced for generations. The Glasgow Pottery in Trenton was first to go in for such ware and engaged artists to work on pieces in their homes before the final glaze. Hand painting was not undertaken at the potteries until about 1880.

Carving in Wood and Stone

*C*arving was a handicraft in colonial and post-Revolutionary New Jersey that took almost equal rank with decorative painting and was employed for similar reasons. Examples of such work, in both wood and stone, are not hard to find, but the identity of the craftsmen has long since been lost, with one or two exceptions.

There were Jerseymen of the eighteenth and early nineteenth century who followed carving as a trade. One of them was Joseph Wright, a resident of Bordentown between 1770 and 1780, of whom previous mention has been made. It is certain, however, that most of the carving was done by men who were first of all craftsmen in other lines and adopted it as a means of decoration. Then, too, there were farmers and villagers who spent the long winter evenings whittling on little articles of household utility and they have left behind some very acceptable work.

Furniture offered an excellent opportunity for carving, and it has been found on chairs, cabinets, dressers, and sofas of Jersey make in walnut, cherry, and bilsted, as well as mahogany. Such articles after the Chippendale, Hepplewhite, Sheraton, and Empire styles were well adapted to such embellishment. In most cases it consisted of the modeled or molded variety. Chests and the old four-poster beds frequently were carved in flat design with leaves and flowers, while small scrolls, leaf veins, and the division of petals were executed in the scratch method.

Jersey cabinetmakers apparently did not resort extensively to carving, but pieces by Egerton and others have enough of such decoration to indicate that they were fairly proficient in the art, even though they resorted most frequently to inlay.

The carving and decorating of wild-fowl decoys was an art form that flourished along the Jersey coast during much of the eighteenth and nineteenth centuries. There are numerous collectors around the country of the old decoys as well as the carvings of birds, wild animals, and persons. Such articles are held in high esteem and are in museums as prized items.

The name of Harry Shourdes, one of New Jersey's master makers of decoys in particular and carvings in general, crops up early in any discussion of such work. As a matter of fact, there are a growing number of hobbyists who duplicate his finest pieces and go on to create original pieces. Aided by power tools, ready-mixed paints, and other conveniences of the present day, their efforts are quite successful and rewarding.

Shourdes was a native of Tuckerton, and his shop in that south Jersey seacoast village was a mecca for hunters in the 1880s and 1890s. Now his decoys are in the Shelbourne Museum and other public, as well as private, collections. He spent a lifetime in the area and became known far and wide. Near the end of his career the demand for more and bigger rigs of decoys grew to such proportions that he was able to keep up with it only by taking on assistants.

Beside meeting the needs of Jerseymen, Shourdes turned out decoys to augment the supply of other makers up and down the Atlantic Coast from Maine to Georgia. He sold many of them to Nathan Cobb, Jr., second-generation member of a Virginia family that made the work a livelihood in the Tidewater. There is a difference in decoys, however, because all the real Cobb decoys are initialed "N" for Nathan or "E" for a brother, Elkenah. The Shourde decoys have the entire name "Cobb" burned across the bottom.

A carving development of the nineteenth century was the wooden Indian adopted by the tobacconist as a symbol of his business. At one time one of them adorned the store front of nearly every such tradesman, but they have disappeared almost completely. One such figure still guards the entrance to a shop in Lambertville and is wheeled inside every night as a precaution against possible theft. The hitching post, so familiar in the horse and buggy days, also has disappeared. Frequently it was carved with the head of a horse or some other figure, with an iron ring to which the reins were fastened.

There was stonecarving in New Jersey, as in the other colonies. Evidence of it remains today in the old date and mile boundary markers, inscriptions and mural designs on old houses, exterior trim at the corners or front entrance, on pillars, and, finally, on headstones and monuments.

The methods followed in stonecarving were very similar to those in wood, and the designs were for the most part cut in rather than raised. Sandstone and limestone were native to this part of the country and were used both for architectural and mortuary work. Occasionally slate was employed for scratch carving, and by the start of the nineteenth century marble, granite, and a little mica stone were available through importation from New England.

The favorite method for dating buildings in New Jersey, particularly through the southern counties, was by the use of a brick design worked into the chimney, or at one end of a structure, but often a cornerstone, cut with the year and name, was set under a gable or into the foundation. The owner of a dwelling erected in 1715 near Scotch Plains told recently of thwarting several attempts that have been made to remove the date stone at night from its place in the lower wall.

Cornices, finial urns, and capitals on the exterior of old

buildings were carved with scrolls and designs. Now and then may be found inscriptions over windows or doorways. Occasionally such carving was in wood, but in such cases the elements and time have combined to destroy it, while the stone work has endured.

As might be expected, the most numerous examples of the early stonecarver's art in New Jersey are to be found among the ancient headstones that mark the resting places of the pioneer dead. All the old graveyards over the state have their quotas of the reddish sandstone and gray-limestone markers bearing quaintly sentimental designs and inscriptions. A great many of the standing stones have lost most of their art because of scaling, while the larger ones, about four by nine feet and covering an entire grave, have been worn smooth by the storms of a century and more beating on them.

The cemetery of St. Mary's Church in Burlington, dating from 1703, those surrounding the Bergen Reformed Church at Jersey City, the old Tennent Church near Freehold, the Baptist Church at Scotch Plains, and many others dating from the early years of the eighteenth century all have ancient stones.

There was a general similarity of design in the early Jersey head and gravestones, but often a marked difference in the quality of lettering and design found on those in different sections. There was not a great deal of travel in those days and usually the stone carver served only adjacent localities. Fortunate was the village that had a competent member of the trade within call, for the others had to be content with men less capable. All in all, the colonial stonecarver with his mallet and his chisels was superior to the average stonecutter of today.

A recently discovered broadside shown to me by a collector of early printing memorabilia is indicative of the versatility of the old stonecutters. Printed by A. Blauvelt in New Brunswick and dated May 13, 1797, it says on behalf of Aaron Ross:

Old Tennent Church

The subscriber begs leave to inform the public that he has taken a shop in New Brunswick, Burnet Street, near the sign of the Leopard, where he proposes carrying on the Stone Cutting business, where all orders for grave, hearth, building stone, etc., etc. will be attended to punctually and the work executed with neatness.

David Jeffries, Ebenezer Price, and J. Tucker were working in northern Jersey as stonecutters prior to the Revolution, according to their names and dates found on stones marking graves in churchyards in Elizabethtown, Orange (New Ark), Union (Connecticut Farms), Woodbridge, Hanover, and Succasunna.

The earliest Jeffries stone in the First Presbyterian Church cemetery, Broad Street, Elizabeth, is dated 1766. It is carved in the same style as those by Price, whose headstone in that graveyard shows that he was born in 1728 and died in 1788.

Price apparently died late in the year, because a notice in the *New Jersey Journal* dated June 4, 1788, sought the whereabouts of "a runaway apprentice, Abner Stewart." The following July a notice over the name of Stewart informed the public that he was a former employee of Price and had opened a shop in Elizabethtown.

Tucker stones dated as early as 1777 have been found in the Presbyterian Church graveyard at Connecticut Farms, long known as Union. A headstone in the old cemetery in Orange marking the grove of Josiah Williams, who died in 1828, has the name of "Schenck, Newark" as the cutter, without further identification. Stones in the same cemetery dated 1831 and 1839 were cut by E. N. Mullin.

Many of the stones dating from the 1760s bear the old symbolism of the Lord's hand appearing from the side, with an ax held firmly, in the act of cutting down a tree. Another style has the decoration at the top enclosed in a semicircle, with an ear of similar shape at either side. Nearly always the face or figure of an angel and sometimes the wings were a part of the design.

The grave, or table, stones were large enough to permit of extensive carving and enough lettering to give quite an account of the rare qualities, or failings, of the deceased. There was room for several angels and their wings might be spread full. The lamb and cherub, sometimes cheerful and then again melancholy of countenance, were other figures. The borders of stones were decorated with bands of fruit, flowers, leaves, or other motifs.

About 1800 the angels, lambs, and cherubs began to disappear and the weeping willow came to be adopted, along with the urn, which had been used occasionally since the 1780s. Probably this resulted from changing religious sentiment as the century of great church building in the state drew to a close and people fell back into a less enthusiastic interest in spiritual things.

Hand carving in stone

Not far from almost every church graveyard, the village stonecarver had his little shop in the old days. The custom has survived to a considerable extent in sections where it has not become so built up that churches are now in the midst of a business area. Some of the firms recall a history of several generations or more, but none of them known to this writer go back to colonial times, and the carver by hand with mallet and chisel has given way to the power cutter.

Some of the carving on headstones in the few remaining family burying grounds to be found in New Jersey is of more than passing interest. It is for the most part of earlier date than that on churchyard stones, and is seemingly just a bit more sentimental. Certainly there is something touching about the little plot, which may be hidden away in a sheltered corner, off the beaten path, usually with towering pines standing guard. Such a place links the present day directly with the early years in the state.

Although there were some attempts at sculpture during the colonial period, the history of this art in the United States really begins with John Frazee, a native Jerseyman, who certainly was the first American sculptor of note. He was born July 18, 1790, on the family farm along the road between Rahway (Bridgeton) and Westfield.

The youngest of ten children of Reuben Frazee, a Revolutionary War veteran, young John early was bound out to a neighboring farmer. He left the farm before he was twenty years of age and went to nearby New Brunswick, where he tried his hand at bricklaying and at waitering in a tavern. In 1813 he married Jane Probasco of Spotswood, New Jersey. A year later an interest in chiseling and whittling, probably resulting from his work as a bricklayer and mason, prompted him to accept work in a stonecutting yard at Haverstraw, New York.

Frazee returned to New Brunswick after several years to set up in business as a stonecutter and soon afterward he shifted activities to New York, with a brother, and later Robert E. Launtis, as a partner. His reputation for making mantels and cutting ornamental steps and headstones spread. He took up residence in what was then the Greenwich Village section of New York and began accepting commissions to execute busts in marble. He had previously made a group figure of his children, prompted by the death of one of them.

Early in the 1820s Frazee joined the U. S. Customs Service at New York and at one period had charge over construction of the Customs House then in course of erection in Wall Street. He was relieved from the post in 1840, but in 1860 Congress ordered payment of $2,868 to his widow as compensation for his services.

During his period of Customs work he found time to model busts of Lafayette when the latter revisited the United States in 1824. Other famous men who sat for him were Benjamin Franklin, Daniel Webster, John Marshall, DeWitt Clinton, and John Jay. In 1834 he was asked to model a series of busts of Boston people to adorn the Athenaeum in that city.

Frazee's first wife died in 1832, leaving five children, and she is buried in the Presbyterian Cemetery at Rahway. His second wife was Lydia Place of New York, whom he married in 1834. He died at the home of a sister in Compton Mills, Rhode Island, on February 24, 1852, as he was putting the finishing touches to a bust of Andrew Jackson.

Princeton University's Museum of Historic Art has acquired the Jackson bust. It had been until then in a private collection since its sale years ago by a niece of Frazee.

The interior and exterior decoration of houses in the eighteenth century furnished a splendid opportunity for Jerseymen with carving ability. Many of the old structures about the state contain today splendid examples of carved work around open fireplaces, over doors and windows, and on staircases. It is quite likely that such work to be found in some of the splendid colonial dwellings along the Delaware River was executed by Joseph Wright. It is definitely

Set of wooden spice boxes

known that he carved the bust of Washington used as the original for the likeness in pottery that until recent years topped the pediment of a large window in the Daniel Hill house near Washington's Crossing.

Georgian architecture was not used in the erection of a great many Jersey structures but, to the extent that it was favored, full advantage was taken of opportunities offered for the woodcarver's art. Some splendid work is to be seen in Morristown, Princeton, and other towns where the English influence was strong. It shows in both exterior and interior ornamentation.

In the days when wooden shipbuilding throve along the Jersey coast, on the Delaware and up the Mullica and other rivers in the southern counties, the carving of figureheads to adorn the vessels was quite an important occupation. Time and expense were lavished on these pieces and they took all manner of form, from the figures of beautiful

Hanging bracket

women to those of sea monsters and birds of the air. Most of these figureheads have disappeared with the ships to the head of which they were once affixed, but occasionally one may be found in an abandoned yard at the water's edge.

The most numerous examples of old-time woodcarving in New Jersey are to be found among articles of domestic necessity. They include the carved hanging spoon racks favored by the Dutch housewives of Monmouth and other counties, and the brush-and-comb holders that hung in sheds.

Weaving, Quilting, and Other Home Arts

*T*he tasks of women in the colonial and post-colonial periods were many. Their days were taken up not only with the performance of those household duties which we usually associate with family life, but with the labor of spinning the yarn, weaving the cloth, and making the home-spun garments quite generally worn in those days.

Women of New Jersey did all those things and, in common with the women in the other colonies, they found time to quilt, knit, and embroider the spreads, samplers, and numerous other articles that are becoming increasingly attractive to collectors. Regardless of social standing, it was regarded as essential to the training of women that they should be proficient in the "fireside arts," and they took a vast pride in their work.

We can only guess that the women in the colony prior to 1700 performed these home arts, because there is not much left in the way of tangible proof. Certainly they had learned them, because such arts were taught in the Old World countries or had been brought across the seas one or two generations before to New England. Then, too, the urge to brighten home surroundings was undoubtedly as strong as it is today.

As life became easier in the eighteenth century, the prac-

A Jersey spinning wheel

tice of the gentler arts extended and the training of girls became a serious matter. This was not left to chance, but instruction was given at home and in seminaries. When it could be afforded, young women were sent away for finishing courses.

The story is told of a maid from Salem who spent a year under tutelage in Philadelphia, and when she returned it was with an embroidered picture as a sort of diploma symbolizing her success.

By the time the nineteenth century arrived, the skill of New Jersey women was far advanced and evidence of their handiwork is quite common. Some of the choicest heirlooms of families old in the state are articles produced by the looms and needles of great-grandmothers and their mothers before them.

The woven coverlets, spreads, and blankets of the colonial and post-colonial periods are as interesting as any of the early decorative art products. Together with the valances and curtains of the old-time four-poster beds, they were objects of concern to every housewife. They were handwoven from materials spun and dyed by the women of the family. Most were made entirely in the home, but around 1800 professional weavers in certain sections were engaged. Some of them maintained stationary looms, while others traveled the countryside from farm to farm. Even earlier was John Lincoln, an ancestor of Abraham Lincoln, who plied his trade in Monmouth County until about 1726, when he moved to Pennsylvania.

Another weaver of colonial times was John Vliet, born at Six-Mile-Run, near New Brunswick, in 1716. He was a fourth-generation descendant from Dirck Van der Vliet, who arrived in Niew Amsterdam (Manhattan) from Holland in 1660. Married to Gretie Wyckoff, a first cousin, he died in 1758 when only forty-two years of age.

From George Vliet, his direct descendant six times removed, I have obtained some of the details of his weaver ancestor. He possesses a copy of his forebear's will, revealing that death came in his prime years.

In 1726 John, the weaver, inherited his father's farm. His eldest son, also John, was born there in 1739 and may also have been a weaver. The second John, at the age of twenty-four years, purchased a farm in Tewksbury Township. After a short time he sold it and bought a farm in Somerset County, where he lived and raised a family until 1880. Then he purchased a farm in Independence Township, Warren County.

"We believe he was a weaver," George Vliet told me, "because he was a close friend of John Honeyman, a weaver, who bought what were later three farms in Somerset County and had a weaving shop."

All the foregoing is confirmed by A. V. D. Honeyman in articles written for the Somerset Historical Society and published in its quarterly magazine several years prior to his death. Unfortunately Honeyman does not dwell on the work of either John Vliet, the weaver, or that of his ancestor. History records, however, that John Honeyman, the spy, was a butcher at Griggstown—a hamlet in Somerset County—and the weaver must have been a son.

According to family tradition both John Vliets, father and son, plied their trade over the countryside from New Brunswick up the Raritan Valley, even into Sussex County, from the 1750s until death took the younger man in the 1800s. The work of neither man has been identified, but spreads, as well as an occasional blanket, which tradition says were woven by one or the other of the Vliets, are to be found. One such spread handed down in the Voorhees family was shown to me a decade ago. In good condition at that time, it was a dull, solid gray in color.

The hand-woven bed covers were made with a foundation of cotton or linen, overshot with wool. The cloth was woven in various lengths and often pieces for coverlets were cut off the same bolt from which garments were made. Women had to be adept at the spinning wheel, dye pot, and loom in those days.

There were few color choices for the old coverlets, mainly because the dyes could not always be obtained. They were restricted mostly to shades of red, blue, yellow, and green or black, but individuality of weaving resulted in a wide variety of combinations. Nuts, wood bark, flowers, leaves, and roots all produced the juices necessary for the desired colors.

During the Revolutionary War the womenfolk of Newark were accustomed to having the wool yarn that they spun woven into blankets by Samuel Conger, who had a shop in Broad Street next to the cabinetmaking establishment of the Bruen Brothers. Another weaver of that period was Josiah Beach, whose home and shop were almost directly across the street, and history records him as being a farmer as well as a weaver.

The entirely homemade bed covers varied in design according to the whim of the maker. Those woven by professional weavers were more symmetrical, and patterns under different names were identified with certain localities. Bearing in mind that coverlets were woven in all parts of the country, we find that among those originating in this state were "New Jersey Dream," "Liberty," "Washington Victory," "Stars and Squares," and "Union."

The Liberty spreads, or blankets, were favorites. They had a floral design, usually in blue or red, and white, and were reversible. Around the border a spread eagle alternated with the word "Liberty," from which the covers got their name. In the lower left corner was woven the name of the person for whom it was made, the date, and the name or initials of the weaver. Thus the one illustrated is identified by the following:

L. Skillman

Millstone

1835

G.W.V.D.

The initials are those of George W. Van Doren, a professional weaver, who had a shop in Millstone, Somerset

Blue and white Liberty blanket

County, beginning around 1830. Another weaver of the period who turned out Liberty blankets was John Stiff of Stillwater in Sussex County. Several of these spreads have been found bearing the date 1836 and one of them, in the possession of a descendant of an Esther Cox, was woven with yarn spun by the good lady from wool sheared off her own sheep.

According to papers of John Budd, a pioneer settler of Chatham, now in the possession of descendants, he was paid ninety-five pounds sterling on December 11, 1730, by Samuel Lum, a weaver from Elizabethtown. Lum bought twenty-seven acres along the Passaic River for that sum and three years later he bought another one hundred acres from Budd, this time for fifty-two pounds sterling. The sales are significant, since the Budds and the Lums have had a profound influence on the town's history.

According to a notice in the *New Jersey Journal* for June 21, 1780, when it was still printed in Chatham, John Donohue conducted "a weaving business at his shop near Nathaniel Bonnell's."

In 1860 "Aunt" Dorcas Day, a weaver of rag carpets, was living in a house at the corner of Passaic and Main Streets in Chatham, according to records from that time. She was said to have woven the carpeting used on stairways and in the bedrooms of most of the homes in the area.

During the forepart of the nineteenth century Nathanial Young was one of the traveling weavers who were familiar over the countryside of what are now Bergen and Hudson counties. His home was in the old town of Bergen, first permanent settlement by the Dutch in New Jersey and long

Varicolored Union blanket

since absorbed into Jersey City. He wove blankets of various designs, including the Liberty, and such a one known to the writer is marked:

Jane Sip
N. Young, Weaver
1838

The lady was a member of the old Bergen family by that name and she spun the yarn of wool from sheep on the Sip farm.

The signing of woven spreads and blankets was quite the custom, followed by women as well as the professional weavers. In Hunterdon County around 1842, Mary Happough made the "Union" cover identified by that word woven around the border and with her own name in the corner. Three colors were used in a variegated block design.

John Cleever is another of the itinerant weavers who traveled the Jersey countryside with their portable looms ever ready to be set up at farmhouses when there was wool for blankets. A native of Easton, on the Pennsylvania side of the Delaware, he apparently spent much of his time on this side of the river, because blankets in several different designs and bearing his name, with a date as late as 1843, have been found in Hunterdon, Warren, and Sussex counties.

John Winans, a member of one of Elizabeth's pioneering families, became a weaver and journeyed as an itinerant over a large area, including present-day Essex, Union, and Middlesex counties, during the 1740s to 1750s.

A number of spreads and blankets woven by Jacob Setzer in the 1840s have been found in Sussex County and even across the Delaware River in Montgomery county. The Blairstown Museum has a Setzer spread made for a Jack Tornacht and dated 1848.

As the making of woven covers became a work for professional weavers, patchwork and piecework quilts gained in popularity among the housewives of the early nineteenth century. These have continued more or less in favor down to the present day. Quilting parties, when neighbors gather to help finish off the spread, are survivals of a custom well over a century old.

Patchwork should not be confused with piecework. In the first instance, pieces of material were sewed onto a foundation of cotton cloth. Piecework consisted of the sewing together of the pieces cut into various sizes and shapes. Calicos, ginghams, and cloth of solid colors were used, and after the patching or piecing had been finished the whole design was made fast in pillow-case fashion to homespun linen. Cotton batting or layers of wool were inserted at the open end and held in place by quilting through from the top to the under side.

The variety of designs in the old patchwork and piecework quilts was limited only by the imagination of the maker. In some instances they were passed around in communities or from mother to daughter, but for the most part women took pride in the fact that each quilt they made was a little different.

The number of woven blankets and patchwork, or piecework, quilts that have survived a century and more of time is surprising. Undoubtedly it is because such articles of handiwork were, in many instances, not used to any great extent by the original owners or makers and as they have been handed down from generation to generation they have been given even greater care.

In the possession of the Union County Historical Society is a patchwork quilt made early in the nineteenth century by women in the Rahway and Willow Grove sections. They belonged to a church sewing circle, and each one who made a little section wrote in ink her name and the date thereon. Other quilts are to be found in the collections about the state, but for the most part they are kept folded carefully in chests or drawers and brought out to be exhibited only on special occasions.

Floor coverings were a luxury for the most part unknown in the homes of New Jersey prior to the nineteenth century, and for that matter unknown in other parts of the country outside of the towns. Of course, rugs and carpets were made for centuries before in the Old World, but they were beyond the means of the early settlers, who were content with sanded floors. Over a large section of this state sand floors were the custom well into the eighteenth century. The ground story of dwellings and the boards of upstair rooms were left bare except for a coating of paint in the upstair rooms.

As houses gained in size and comfort, housewives had the desire to cover the wide boards laid for floors. There was not only a bareness about them, but drafts made living in the long winters a matter of strong discomfort. Thus the making of handworked rugs and carpets came in as one of the tasks of colonial women.

There was a limited amount of weaving, but by far the greater portion of rugs and carpets were hand worked. It was not until close to the middle of the nineteenth century that factory production was of any consequence.

Rag rugs were made in New Jersey more widely than other types. They had little decorative value and variety of design was obtained by the use of different-colored material. The usual process was to cut cloth into long strips for braiding. These pieces then were sewed together in a circular or oval design, starting from the center. They were of various dimensions and usually were placed in front of open hearths, in front of chairs or at other places where there was a great amount of wear.

When the itinerant and community weavers became known, women were well accustomed to accumulating worn-out apparel and other material for weaving into carpet strips. These strips were used to cover entirely the floors of bedchambers and some other rooms in the house.

Hooked rugs in the "hook and pull through" method were made to a limited extent in New Jersey after the manner taught by settlers who moved in from New England. Canvas, hemp, or burlap was used as a foundation. It was stretched on a wooden frame and the design or pattern worked in by inserting a wood-handled steel needle or hook up and down through the material. Pieces of wool yarn or strips of rags were used; afterward the top ends were clipped or cut to produce a chenille effect. The wearing quality of the rug depended upon the weight of the pieces and the tightness with which they were worked in and out of the base.

Hooked rugs have never entirely lost their charm. In colonial times they were simple and followed a few general designs in the form of squares, circles, and other variations. Some of those of Jersey origin prior to the Revolution featured scrolls, flowers, and leaves. By the time 1800 arrived, animals and birds had been added and later ships, flags, and patriotic or historical subjects were popular.

Rugs and carpets were uncommon enough in colonial New Jersey that they were mentioned in household inventories along with covers woven or hand-worked for chairs and tables. One or two instances are on record of specific mention of rugs, minutely described as to colors and design, which were willed to surviving relatives.

The products of home arts thus far discussed are in the decorative class, but that is mainly because they were made so in meeting a more or less utilitarian necessity. Obviously there was a greater enjoyment and even recreation in needlework for the women who lived a century and more ago. During winter evenings by the fireside, when the day's work was done, they turned to such lighter tasks.

Early decorative needlework included samplers, chair covers, fire screens, dresser and mirror tops, bags, purses, towels, scarves, and various articles of clothing adorned with embroidery or fine stitching. Many a party dress or wedding gown is cherished today because of the carefully executed work.

Samplers have been chosen for discussion because, as the word implies, they were examples of a style or design and served to show what skill the maker possessed. Although not in the same form, samplers were known abroad from early times and were brought to this country by the first settlers. In the seventeenth century they were frequently a yard or more in length and a foot wide, with stitching or embroidery thereon as a pattern for reference. Along toward 1700, to which period the earliest specimens of New Jersey origin are traced, they had shrunk to smaller dimensions and verses and figures had begun to be done.

As if to lend weight to the name by which they are known, many of the old samplers bear evidence of the handiwork of young children. They displayed letters of the alphabet and figures of man or beast. Frequently the name of the maker and the date were indicated. Even in grand-mother's time, the acceptable completion of such a sampler was proof of ability to undertake more exacting work.

Samplers continued to be favorite objects of handiwork among New Jersey women well into the nineteenth century. Nearly every home had framed specimens hung on the walls. Those bearing religious quotations were made through all the years, and for that reason are difficult to identify as to period except when dated. Others were of pictorial de-sign, or represented contemporary events in history, so that it is possible to place them with reasonable accuracy. Thus we know that those bearing the likeness of Washington are probably of the late eighteenth century and those showing a steamboat, of the 1820s. Sampler houses, beasts and birds, fruits, flowers, and maps were other subjects.

Rough canvas, coarse linen, or ordinary homespun were used for samplers. Both woolen yarn and silk thread were used in a variety of stitches, with cross-stitching used more than any of the others. Bright colors were the order, and letters or numerals were worked alternately in red, blue, or green. Only in the more elaborate pictorial samplers was there a blending of the different hues.

Embroidered pictures were later and really a step ad-vanced from samplers. They were a form of decorative art that flourished during the latter years of the eighteenth

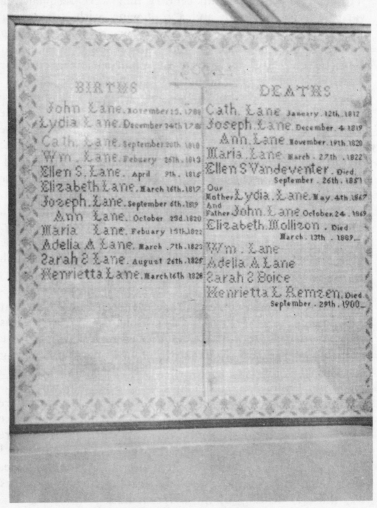

Genealogical sampler

century over into the nineteenth and often were worked in such detail that they became almost objects of art. Like samplers, they were framed for hanging, but this was done with more elaboration and the entire surface was covered with glass to prevent dust or causing damage from handling.

Every subject that might appeal to the individual fancy in the way of flowers and fruits, landscapes, maps, figures of both man and beast, houses, and biblical scenes were worked on a background of silk, linen, or canvas cloth. A variety of stitches was used and the silken thread carefully blended as to color and shade. A realistic touch sometimes was added by the use of human hair on the heads of figures, while the face, arms, and legs were painted. In one Middlesex county home there is carefully preserved an embroidered picture of flowers made about 1830 entirely from hair, ranging in color from red and brown to white.

The death of Washington was a signal for New Jersey women to honor his memory by making embroidered pictures of which his likeness was the central theme. After his long stays in this state during the years of the Revolution, he was held in particularly high esteem by its citizens. Judging from the uniformity of design found on such pictures, it is a not-unlikely assumption that the idea for them may have been fostered by merchants who sold tracings with the floss or twisted silk thread.

Other historic events prompted embroidered pictures, and the detail with which they often were executed undoubtedly means many months of work, probably stretching into years. Some of those pictures found framed but not entirely completed is indication that death overtook the maker before her task was finished.

Embroidery on articles of apparel does not hold much interest for the present-day collector of the early New Jersey decorative arts, but it was of considerable importance in the time of flowery waistcoats and satin jackets. In the colonial period of powdered wigs and lace collars, gentlemen were not averse to having embroidered work on the cuffs and lapels of their best clothes.

Gradually such ornamentation became outmoded for men, but the womenfolk continued to use embroidery on dresses and undergarments. As might be expected in such a personal matter, some of the most skillful work of that sort is to be found on such articles.

Handmade lace was another accomplishment of this state's pioneer women, and even after the advent of the machine it continued to be made. It is extremely doubtful, however, if lacemaking was ever on a commercial basis. That was left to the immigrants from England's midland counties, around Ipswich and Nottingham, who settled in New England and sent peddlers into New York and New Jersey to sell "pillow lace" produced with the use of bamboo bobbins.

Only a few instances have been recorded where lacemaking was undertaken seriously by the women of New Jersey. They did not take to the bobbin or frame and used the needle almost entirely to make straight lace, without figures, for trimming pillow edges, bed canopies, baby clothes, and their own articles of apparel. It was made in long pieces and kept rolled up for the cutting off of pieces as required.

Early in the nineteenth century a form of lace was made by tatting, in which linen thread, wound on a small shuttle held in one hand, was woven in and out and up and over to produce endless chain or circular designs. This tatting was useful not only as edging on garments, pillow cases, and doilies, but whole spreads or covers were made with intricate designs by first doing small pieces and afterward sewing them together. In some Jersey families tatting has been taught from one generation to another, but the knack it requires is known to only a few nowadays.

For no particular reason, knitting has been left to last for discussion. As a matter of fact, it was a home craft practised as a necessity, and the decorative element was a second consideration. Long, severe winters in poorly heated houses called for warm clothing over most of the state. Socks, hats, mufflers, and even shirts were knit by the women from yarn made from the wool of sheep raised often on the same farm.

During the Revolution New Jersey women knit clothing for the ill-clad troops when they were in winter encampment at Jockey Hollow and Camp Middlebrook. In the diary of Martha Washington kept during her stay at the Ford Mansion in Morristown, there are several entries of occasions when she was joined in her knitting by women of the town.

Scarcely any of those old knitted articles have survived the ravages of time, but in a few instances cedar chests, camphor, and unusual care have combined to preserve examples of such things. There are also the heavy knitted comforters that were the forerunners of the more modern brightly colored afghan, and, rarest of all, the shawl or robe that was wrapped around the shoulders to protect against the cold on long wintry rides.

Taken all in all, the "fireside" crafts of early New Jersey are interesting as well as important to study. The women of today may learn much from the skill and patience that were requisites. Then, too, an excellent idea of living conditions in those times is to be gleaned from such research.

Appendix: List of State's Early Craftsmen

1. CABINETMAKERS
Note: w. before a date indicates "actively working."

Aikman, Thomas, Burlington, Burlington Co., w. 1800

Britten, Elihu, Elizabethtown, Essex Co., w. 1805–1830

Bruen, Caleb, Newark, Essex Co., w. 1796

Bruen, Mathias, Newark, Essex Co., w. 1796

Burroughs, Caleb, Madison, Morris Co., w. 1820

Egerton, Mathew, New Brunswick, Middlesex Co., w. 1767–1802

Egerton, Mathew, Jr., New Brunswick, Middlesex Co., w. 1785–1837

Gray, Richardson, Elizabethtown, Essex Co., b. 1754—d. 6/21/1818

Kerwood, William, Trenton, Mercer Co., w. 1808

Mann, John, Elizabethtown & Newark, Essex Co., b. 12/9/1770—d. 5/1/1831

Meeker & Clarkson, Rahway (Bridge Town), Essex Co., w. 1822

Moore, Alexander, New Brunswick, Middlesex Co., w. 1730

Nichols, Robert, Newark, Essex Co., w. 1760

Parsell, Oliver, New Brunswick, Middlesex Co., b. 1757—d. 5/18/1818

Phyfe, Duncan, New Market, Middlesex Co., w. 1815

Randolph, Benjamin, Burlington Co., w. 1777–1798

Ryckman, John, New Brunswick, Middlesex Co., w. 1793

Rousett, Abraham, Elizabethtown, Essex Co., b. 1780—d. 1815

Rousett & Mulford, Elizabethtown, Essex Co., w. 1807

Scudder, John, Rahway, Essex Co., w. 1780–1810

Topping, James, Chester, Morris Co., b. 1820—d. 1874

Willets, William, Lamington, Somerset Co., w. 1785–1810

Williams, Ichabod, Elizabethtown, Essex Co., b. 1768—d. 1837

2. CLOCKMAKERS

Baker, Samuel, New Brunswick, Middlesex Co., w. 1822–1858

Baldwin, Mathias, Elizabeth, Essex Co., b. 1795

Brokaw, Aaron, Rahway (Bridge Town), Essex Co., w. 1780–1810

Brokaw, Cornelius, Rahway, Essex Co., w. 1785–1815

Brokaw, John, Rahway (Bridge Town), Essex Co., w. 1806

Brokaw, Isaac, Rahway (Bridge Town), Essex Co., b. 1746—d. 1826

Budd, Joseph, Mount Holly, Burlington Co., w. 1760

Burnet, Smith, Newark, Essex Co., w. 1794

Cleveland, Benjamin Norton, Newark, Essex Co., b. 1767—d. 1837

Cooper, Isaac, Woodbury, Gloucester Co., w. 1832

Coppuck, George Washington, Mount Holly, Burlington Co., w. 1825

Crow, William, Salem, Salem Co., w. 1725–1740

Dickinson, Richard, Mount Holly, Burlington Co., w. 1780

Dawes, William P., Elizabethtown, Essex Co., w. 1805–1814

Dowling, G. R. & B. Co., Newark, Essex Co., w. 1832

Ely, Hugh, Trenton, Mercer Co., b. 1783—d. 1829

Emmons, Erastus, Trenton, Mercer Co., w. 1807

Fling, Daniel, Mount Holly, Burlington Co., w. 1790

Gamage, Samuel, Elizabeth, Essex Co., b. 4/16/1782—d. 1824

Giles, Joseph, Trenton, Mercer Co., w. 1804

Gould, Uriah, Mendham, Morris Co.

Hacker, Michael, Tewksbury, Hunterdon Co., d. 1796

Hill, Joachim, Flemington, Hunterdon Co., b. 1783—d. 1869

Hill, Peter, Mount Holly, Burlington Co., w. 1760

Hollinshead, George, Woodstown, Burlington Co., w. 1820

Hollinshead, Hugh, Mount Holly, Burlington Co., b. 1753

Hollinshead, Jacob, Salem, Salem Co., w. 1772

Hollinshead, Job, Haddonfield, Camden Co.

Hollinshead, John, Burlington, Burlington Co., b. 1745

Hollinshead, Joseph, Burlington, Burlington Co., w. 1740

Hollinshead, Joseph, Jr., Burlington, Burlington Co., w. 1751

Hollinshead, Morgan, Moorestown, Burlington Co., b. 1757

Hooley, Richard, Flemington, Hunterdon Co., w. 1796

Hudson, Edward, Mount Holly, Burlington Co., w. 1775–1790

Hudson, William, Mount Holly, Burlington Co., w. 1773–1789

Hurtin & Burgi, Bound Brook, Somerset Co., w. 1766–1780

Huston, James, Trenton, Mercer Co., w. 1807

Lane, Aaron, Elizabethtown, Essex Co., w. 1780–1814

Lane, Andrew, Elizabethtown, Essex Co.

Leslie, William J., Trenton, Mercer Co., b. 1739—d. 1831
Lupp (Leupp), Peter, New Brunswick, Middlesex Co., b. 1797—
    d. 1827
Lyon, Richard, Elizabethtown, Essex Co., w. 1799
Maus, Jacob, Trenton, Mercer Co., w. 1779
Miller, Aaron, Elizabethtown, Essex Co., w. 1747–1770
Miller, Kennedy, Elizabethtown, Essex Co., w. 1765
Newton, J. L., Trenton, Mercer Co., w. 1804
Nicholl, John, Belvedere, Warren Co., w. 1825–1860
Parry, John, Trenton, Mercer Co., w. 1799
Pearson, Isaac, Burlington, Burlington Co., w. 1720
Pearson & Hollinshead, Burlington, Burlington Co., w. 1740
Probasco, John, Trenton, Mercer Co., w. 1778
Pressaq, John, Rahway, Union Co., w. 1827
Rea, George, Flemington, Hunterdon Co., b. 1774—d. 1838
Reed, Isaac, New Brunswick, Middlesex Co., w. 1798
Reeve, Benjamin, Greenwich, Cumberland Co., b. 1750—d. 1790
Sayre, Elias, Pleasant Valley, Monmouth Co., w. 1805
Shoemaker, David, Mt. Holly, Burlington Co., w. 1760
Shourds, Samuel, Bordentown, Burlington Co., w. 1740
Wheeler, Charles, New Brunswick, Middlesex Co., w. 1798
Whitehead, John, Woodbury, Gloucester Co., w. 1750
Williams, Thomas, Flemington, Hunterdon Co., w. 1796
Willis, John, Burlington, Burlington Co., w. 1748
Woodruff, Ezra, Elizabethtown, Union Co., w. 1808–1817
Yates, Joseph, Trenton, Mercer Co., w. 1789–1803

3. CHAIRMAKERS

Alling, David, Newark, Essex Co., w. 1825–1836
Boden, Omar, Burlington Co., b. 1762—d. 1844
Chambers, Alexander, Trenton, Mercer Co., w. 1763–1780
Clayton, Samuel, Allentown, Monmouth Co., w. 1810
Dunham, Campbell, New Brunswick, Middlesex Co., w. 1802
Davidson, Herbert, Englishtown, Monmouth Co., w. 1820
Claever, Henryk, Crosswicks, Burlington Co., w. 1690–1710
Leonard, John, Englishtown, Monmouth Co., w. 1815
Mitchell, Isaac, Elizabethtown, Essex Co., w. 1789–1810
Moon, Samuel, Morrisville, Mercer Co., w. 1805
Randolph, Benjamin, Burlington Co., w. 1777–1798
Ryckman, John, New Brunswick, Middlesex Co., w. 1793

Thompson, Pierson, Englishtown, Monmouth Co., w. 1815

Whitehead, David, Elizabethtown, Essex Co., w. 1800–1818, d. 9/18/1844

Woodruff, John, Elizabethtown, Essex Co., w. 1795–1825

4. SILVERSMITHS AND JEWELERS

Baker, Elias, New Brunswick, w. 1827

Baldwin, S. M. & Co., Newark, w. 1850

Bingham, John, Salem, w. 1640

Boudinot, 3d, Elias, Princeton & Elizabethtown, b. 1706—d. 1770

Burnet, Smith, Newark, w. 1794

Byrne, James & Co., Elizabethtown, w. 1799

Cleveland, Benjamin, Newark, b. 1767—d. 1837

Coleman, Benjamin, Burlington, w. 1785

Coleman, Nathaniel, Burlington, w. 1776

Coleman, Samuel, Burlington, w. 1805

Darby, Elias, Elizabethtown, 1830

Dickerson, John, Morristown, 1755–1828

Downing & Phelps, Newark, w. 1810

Dunn, Cary, Morristown & Newark, w. 1767–1782

Dunscombe, Dennis, Elizabethtown, w. 1782–1788

Durand & Co., Newark, w. 1850

Durand, Cyrus, Newark, b. 1787—d. 1868

Fireng, J. P., Burlington, w. 1810

Fitch, John, Trenton, w. 1769–1775

Halsted, Benjamin, Newark & Elizabethtown, w. 1764–1783

Hayes & Cotton, Newark, w. 1831

Hetzel, John M., Newton, w. 1795

Hinsdale, Epaphras, Newark, w. 1801

Howell, Silas, New Brunswick, Middlesex Co., w. 1794–1798

Hurton, Joshua, Newark, Essex Co., w. 1735–1765

Lane, Aaron, Elizabethtown, Essex Co., 1753–1819

Lane, Andrew, Elizabethtown, Essex Co., w. 1780–1815

Lewis, Isaac, Newark, Essex Co., w. 1782

Lupp (Leupp), Charles, New Brunswick, Middlesex Co., b. 1788—d. 1825

Lupp (Leupp), Henry, New Brunswick, Middlesex Co., w. 1783

Lupp (Leupp), Louis, New Brunswick, Middlesex Co., w. 1800

Lupp (Leupp), Peter, New Brunswick, Middlesex Co., b. 1787—d. 1827

Lupp (Leupp), V., New Brunswick, Middlesex Co., d. 1805
Lupp (Leupp), William, New Brunswick, w. 1820–1837
Maus, Jacob, Trenton, Mercer Co., w. 1781–1782
Paxson & Hayes, Newark, Essex Co., w. 1845
Pearson, Isaac, Burlington, Burlington Co., w. 1748
Reeder, Abner, Trenton, Mercer Co., b. 1766—d. 1841
Reeves, Stephen, Burlington, Burlington Co., 1767
Richards, Stephen, Cohansey Bridge (Bridgeton), Cumberland Co.,
    w. 1769
Richardson, Enow & Co., Newark, Essex Co., w. 1835
Robinson, Anthony, Trenton, Mercer Co., w. 1788
Rodman, Thomas, Burlington, Burlington Co., w. 1748–1765
Schenck, John, Pleasant Valley, Monmouth Co., w. 1792
Stout, Samuel, Princeton, Mercer Co., w. 1779–1794
Syng, Philip, Sr., Cape May, Cape May Co., w. 1723
Taylor & Baldwin, Newark, Essex Co., w. 1820
Thomas, William, Elizabethtown, Essex Co., & Trenton, Mercer
    Co., w. 1779–1780
Van Buren, William, Newark, Essex Co., w. 1792
Van Voorhees, Daniel, Princeton, Mercer Co., b. 1751—d. 1824
Williams, Benjamin, Elizabethtown, Essex Co., w. 1788–1794
Wilson, James, Trenton, Mercer Co., b. 1749—d. 1834
Yates, Joseph, Trenton, Mercer Co., w. 1793–1798

5. GLASSMAKERS

Atlantic Glass Works, Batsto, Burlington Co., 1852–1857
Bacon, Edward, Clayton, Gloucester Co., 1851–1856
Bainford, John, Camden, Camden Co., 1841–1842
Becket, Benjamin, Clayton, Gloucester Co., 1850
Bodine, Joel E. & Co., Bridgeton, Cumberland Co., 1846
Buck, John P., Bridgeton, Cumberland Co., 1836
Burling Bros., Batsto, Burlington Co., 1858–1859
Capewell, John & James, Camden, Camden Co., 1841–1857
Capewell Glass Works, Camden, Camden Co., 1841–1857
Carpenter, Thomas, Bridgeton, Cumberland Co., 1784
Clementon, Samuel, Clementon, Camden Co., 1800
Clementon Glass Works, Clementon, Camden Co., 1820–1825
Cochran's Glass Works, Medford, Gloucester Co., 1842
Coffin, William, Green Bank, Burlington Co., 1840
Cohansay Glass Works, Bridgeton, Cumberland Co., 1870

Columbia Glass Works, Medford, Gloucester Co., 1842
Crowley, Samuel, Bulltown, Burlington Co., 1858–1870
Crowleytown Glass Works, Batsto, Burlington Co., 1851
Dennisville Glass Works, Dennis Creek, Cape May Co., 1868
Eagle Glass Works, Pt. Elizabeth, Cumberland Co., 1810
Excelsior Glass Works, Camden, Camden Co., 1845–1857
Fislerville Glass Works, Clayton, Gloucester Co., 1850
Fisler, Jacob, Clayton, Gloucester Co., 1850–1856
Free Will Glass Works, Williamstown, Camden Co., 1835
Getzinger & Rosenbaum, Estellville, Atlantic Co., 1868–1875
Haines, Jonathan, Clementon, Camden Co., 1800
Harmony Glass Works, Glassboro, Gloucester Co., 1813
Heston & Carpenter, Bridgeton, Cumberland Co., 1786
Heston, Col. Thomas, Bridgeton, Cumberland Co., 1783
Isabella Glass Works, Old Brooklyn, Camden Co., 1848–1867
Jersey City Glass Works, Jersey City, Hudson Co., 1824
Jersey City Flint Glass Works, Jersey City, Hudson Co., 1861
Lewisville & Temperanceville Glass Works, Glassboro, Gloucester
    Co., 1834
Lippencott, Wisham & Co., Milford, Burlington Co., 1852
Malaga Glass Works, Malaga, Gloucester Co., 1814
Marshalville Glass Works, Tuckahoe, Gloucester Co., 1810
Milford Glass Works, Milford, Burlington Co., 1838–1852
Moore Bros., Clayton, Gloucester Co., 1856–1880
Moore, John M., Clayton, Gloucester Co., 1856–1880
Old Brooklyn Glass Works, Old Brooklyn, Camden Co., 1838–1852
Olive Glass Works, Glassboro, Gloucester Co., 1781
Pt. Elizabeth Glass Works, Pt. Elizabeth, Cumberland Co., 1799
Potter & Bodine, Bridgeton, Cumberland Co., 1857
Potter, David, Bridgeton, Cumberland Co., 1857
Rink, John, Glassboro, Gloucester Co., 1813–1823
Reed & Moulds, Jersey City, Hudson Co., 1855
Rosenbaum, John G., Bridgeton, Cumberland Co., 1843
Sasockson Glass Works, Camden Co., 1850
Scott, John H. & Daniel, Estelleville, Atlantic Co., 1825–1844
Sharp, Alexander H., Estelleville, Atlantic Co., 1845–1856
Stanger, Solomon, Daniel, Adam, Christian, Francis, Peter & Philip,
    Salem, Salem Co. & Glassboro, Gloucester Co., 1780–1810
Stratton, Nathaniel, Bridgeton, Cumberland Co., 1836
Tice, Clayton, Old Brooklyn, Camden Co., 1857–1868
Tonkin & Carpenter, Glassboro, Gloucester Co., 1784–1785

Tonkin, Samuel, Glassboro, Gloucester Co., 1784–1785
Wapler's Glass Works, Green Bank, Burlington Co., 1840–1850
Warrick, Woodward, Glassboro, Gloucester Co., 1841–1883
Whitney & Warrick, Glassboro, Gloucester Co., 1841–1883
Whitney Bros., Glassboro, Gloucester Co., 1837–1882
Whitney Glass Works, Glassboro, Gloucester Co., 1887
Wistar, Casper, Salem, Salem Co., 1737–1752

6. POTTERY AND CHINA MAKERS

American Art China Works, Trenton, Mercer Co., 1891
American Porcelain Mfg. Co., Gloucester, Gloucester Co., 1854
American Pottery Co., Jersey City, Hudson Co., 1833
Atcheson & Co., Newark, Essex Co., 1854
Beerbower, L. B. & Co., Elizabethtown, Essex Co., 1879
Bloor, Ott & Booth, Trenton, Mercer Co., 1860
Broome, Isaac, Trenton, Mercer Co., 1880
Burroughs & Mountford Co., Trenton, Mercer Co., 1879
Carr, Jas. & Co., So. Amboy, Middlesex Co., 1870
Ceramic Art Co., Trenton, Mercer Co., 1889
Congress Hill Pottery, So. Amboy, Middlesex Co., 1810
Cook Pottery Co., Trenton, Mercer Co., 1894
Coxe, John, New England Town, Cape May Co., 1684
Coxon & Co., Trenton, Mercer Co., 1863
Crescent Pottery Co., Trenton, Mercer Co., 1881
DeCasse, Woodbridge, Middlesex Co., 1842
Delaware Pottery Co., Trenton, Mercer Co., 1884
Durrell, Philip, Elizabethtown, Essex Co., 1779
Eagle Pottery, Perth Amboy, Middlesex Co., 1858
Empire Pottery, Trenton, Mercer Co., 1863
Enterprise Pottery, Trenton, Mercer Co., 1880
East Trenton Pottery Works, Trenton, Mercer Co., 1888
Fell & Thropp Co., Trenton, Mercer Co.
Fish, Chas. & Co., So. Amboy, Middlesex Co., 1868
Fulper Pottery Co., Flemington, Hunterdon Co., 1805
Gillig, Daniel, Newark, Essex Co., 1850
Glasgow Pottery Co., Trenton, Mercer Co., 1863
Gould, Capt. Thomas, Caldwell, Essex Co., 1840
Greenwood Pottery Co., Trenton, Mercer Co., 1861
Halsey, Ichabod, Elizabethtown, Essex Co., 1783
Hill, Samuel, Flemington, Hunterdon Co., 1772–1783
Homer & Shirley, New Brunswick, Middlesex Co., 1830

Hunt, Robert, Elizabethtown, Essex Co., 1780
International Pottery Co., Trenton, Mercer Co., 1860
Krumeich, Balthasar, Newark, Essex Co., 1837
Jersey City Pottery Co., Jersey City, Hudson Co., 1825–1850
Mackay, Cap. Ephraim, New Brunswick, Middlesex Co., 1810
Maddock, Thos. & Sons, Trenton, Mercer Co., 1859
Maddock Pottery Co., Trenton, Mercer Co., 1893
Maddock, John & Sons, Trenton, Mercer Co., 1894
Mann, John, Rahway, Essex Co., w. 1820s
McCully, John S., Trenton, Mercer Co., 1779
Mercer Pottery Co., Trenton, Mercer Co., 1868
Millington & Asbury, Trenton, Mercer Co., 1857
Newark Pottery, Newark, Essex Co., 1862
New Jersey Porcelain & Earthenware Co., Jersey City, Hudson Co., 1825
New Jersey Pottery Co., Trenton, Mercer Co., 1869
Poillon & Weidner, Woodbridge, Middlesex Co., 1867
Pruden, Elizabethtown, Essex Co., 1835
Raisner, Joseph, Lambertsville, Mercer Co., 1848
Rhodes & Yates, Trenton, Mercer Co., 1858
Rouse & Turner, Jersey City, Hudson Co., 1850
Rue, John L. & Co., South Amboy, Middlesex Co., 1870
Salamander Pottery, Woodbridge, Middlesex Co., 1825
Snowden, Richard, Haddonfield, Camden Co., 1830
Star Porcelain Co., Trenton, Mercer Co.
Swan Hill Pottery, South Amboy, Middlesex Co., 1866
Taylor & Speeler, Trenton, Mercer Co., 1852
Trenton China Co., Trenton, Mercer Co., 1859
Trenton Pottery Co., Trenton, Mercer Co., 1865
Ware & Letts, South Amboy, Middlesex Co., 1806
Willis & Steel, Elizabethtown, Essex Co., 1797–1800
Wingender, Chas. & Bros., Haddonfield, Camden Co.
Wiseman, Jas. & Co., South Amboy, Middlesex Co., 1868
Young, Astbury & Maddock, Trenton, Mercer Co., 1873
Young, Wm. & Sons, Trenton, Mercer Co., 1855

7. MARKS OF NEW JERSEY POTTERIES

Key to plate numbers appearing on the pages immediately following:

Founded

1–8 The Jersey City Pottery, Jersey City   1829
     D. & J. Henderson

		Founded
	American Pottery Mfg. Co.	1833
9	William Young & Sons, Trenton	1853
10–17	The Willets Mfg. Co., Trenton	1879
18	The City Pottery Co., Trenton	1859
19–25	Greenwood Pottery Co., Trenton	1861
26–28	East Trenton Pottery Co., Trenton	1888
29–30	Millington, Astbury & Poulson, Trenton	1853
31–32	Thos. Maddock & Sons, Trenton	1859
33	Thos. Maddock's Sons Co., Trenton	1902
34–36	The Maddock Pottery Co., Trenton	1893
37–40	John Maddock & Sons, Trenton	1894
41–68	The Glasgow Pottery	1863
69–80	Ott & Brewer, Trenton	1863
81–88	The Cook Pottery Co., Trenton	1894
89–91	Isaac Broome, Trenton	1880
92	Coxon & Co., Trenton	1863
93	Trenton Pottery Co., Trenton	1865
94–109	Mercer Pottery Co., Trenton	1865
110	New Jersey Pottery Co., Trenton	1869
111–128	Inter'l Pottery Co., Trenton	1860
128–131	American Crockery Co., Trenton	1876
131–137	Burroughs & Mountford Co., Trenton	1879
138–142	Prospect Hill Pottery Co., Trenton	1880
143–149, 155	Anchor Pottery Co., Trenton	1894
150–151	Delaware Pottery, Trenton	1884
152–165	Crescent Pottery, Trenton	1881
166–168	Empire Pottery, Trenton	1863
169	Enterprise Pottery, Trenton	1880
170–179	Trenton Potteries Co., Trenton	1892
180	The Bellmark Pottery Co., Trenton	1893
181–183	The Fell & Thropp Co., Trenton	
184–185	The Trenton Pottery Works, Trenton	
186	Keystone Pottery Works, Trenton	
187	Star Porcelain Co., Trenton	
188–192	The Ceramic Art Co., Trenton	1889
193	The Trenton China Co., Trenton	1859
194	The American Art China Works, Trenton	1891
195–196	Columbian Art Pottery, Trenton	
197, 201	L. B. Beerbower & Co., Elizabeth	1816
198	Chas. Wingender & Bros., Haddonfield	
199	C. L. & H. A. Poillon, Woodbridge	
200	American Porcelain Mfg. Co., Gloucester	1854

Marks of New Jersey potteries

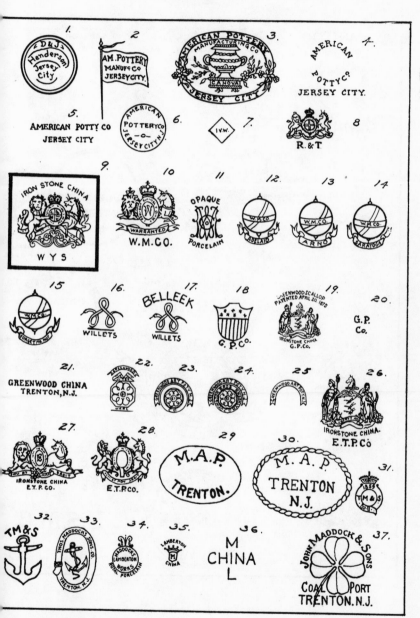

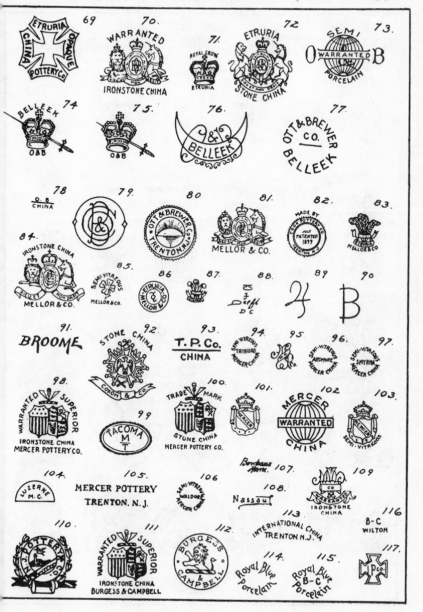

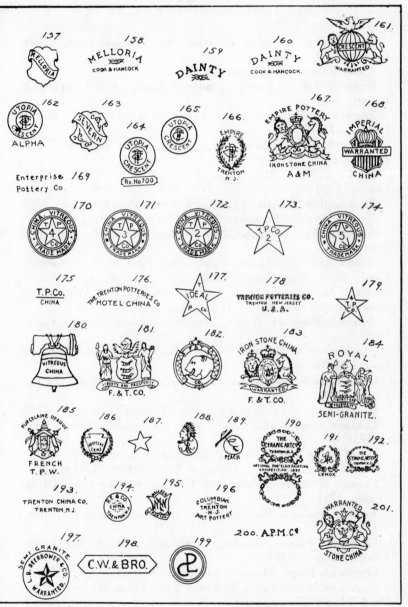

157

158. MELLORIA
COOK & HANCOCK

159 DAINTY

160 DAINTY
COOK & HANCOCK.

161. CRESCENT WARRANTED

162 UTOPIA CRESCENT
ALPHA

163 SEVERN

164 UTOPIA CRESCENT
Rd. No 700

165. UTOPIA CRESCENT

166. EMPIRE TRENTON N.J.

167. EMPIRE POTTERY
IRONSTONE CHINA
A & M

168. IMPERIAL WARRANTED CHINA

Enterprise Pottery Co. 169

170 CHINA VITREOUS 4 T P Co TRADE MARK

171 CHINA VITREOUS 3 T P Co TRADE MARK

172 CHINA VITREOUS 2 T P Co TRADE MARK

173. T P Co 2

174. CHINA VITREOUS 5 T P Co TRADE MARK

175 T.P.Co. CHINA

176. THE TRENTON POTTERIES Co HOTEL CHINA

177. T IDEAL P Co

178 TRENTON POTTERIES CO. TRENTON NEW JERSEY U.S.A.

179. T.P. Co.

180 VITREOUS CHINA

181. LIBERTY AND PROSPERITY F. & T. CO.

182. F. & T. Co.

183 IRON STONE CHINA WARRANTED F. & T. CO.

184 ROYAL SEMI-GRANITE.

185 PORCELAINE OPAQUE FRENCH T.P.W.

186 UTOPIA CHINA

187. ★

188.

189. PEACH

190 THE CERAMIC ART Co TRENTON N.J. NATIONAL PORCELAIN PAINTING COMPETITION 1887

191 LENOX

192 THE CERAMIC ART Co TRENTON N.J.

193 TRENTON CHINA CO. TRENTON, N.J.

194. F.F. & CO. CHINA TRENTON

195. MILLER N.W.

196 COLUMBIAN TRENTON N.J. ART POTTERY

201. WARRANTED STONE CHINA

200. A.P.M.Cº

197. SEMI GRANITE L.B. BEERBOWER & CO. WARRANTED ★

198. C.W. & BRO.

199

8. FORGES AND FURNACES

Andover Iron Works or Waterloo Forge, Pequest River, Sussex County, 1760

Atsion Furnace, Burlington County, 1755

Batsto or Batstow Furnace, branch of Mullica River, Burlington County, 1767

Beman's or White Meadow Forge, Rockaway River, Morris County, 1753

Birmingham and Retreat Forge, north branch Rancocas Creek, Burlington County, 1800

Black's Creek or Bordentown Forge, Black Creek, Burlington County, 1800

Bloomingdale Furnace, Pequannock River, Passaic County, 1765

Boonton Works, Rockaway River, Morris County, 1770

Brooklyn Forge or Works, Musconetcong Creek, Morris County, 1764

Budd's Iron Works or Cumberland Furnace, Manusnershin Creek, Cumberland County, 1810

Burnt Meadow Forge or John Harriman's Iron Works, east branch of Rockaway River, Morris County, 1750

Butcher's Forge or Works, Metedeconk River, Ocean County, 1808

Changewater or Robeson's Forge, Musconetcong Creek, Warren County, 1750

Charlotteburg Furnace and Forges, Pequannock River, Passaic County, 1767

Chelsea Forge, Musconetcong Creek, Warren County, 1751–1753

Cohansie Iron Works, Cedar Creek, Cumberland County, prior to 1753

Dover Forge, Dover Forge Pond, Ocean County, 1830

Etna Furnace or Forge, Tuckahoe River, Atlantic County, 1815

Ferrago or Bomber Forge and Furnace, Bomber Lake, Ocean County, 1811

Franklin Furnace, Norman's Pond, Hardystone, Sussex County, 1765

Gloucester Furnace, Landing Creek, part of Little Egg River, Atlantic County, 1813

Greenwich Forge, Musconetcong River, Warren County, 1750

Guinea or Muir's Forge, Rockaway River below White Meadow Pond, Morris County, before 1774

Hacklebarney or Budd's Forge, Falls of Lamington, Pottersville, Hunterdon County, 1763

Hamburg Forge and Furnace or Iron Works, Wallkill River, Sussex County, 1792

Hampton Furnace and Forge, junction of Robber's Run and Batsto River, Burlington County, 1795

Hanover Furnace, Rancocas Creek near Brown's Mills, Burlington County, 1791

Hibernia or Adventure Furnace and Forge, Whippany River, Morris County, 1763

Jackson's Forge and Dover Furnace or Iron Works, Jackson's Brook, Randolph, Morris County, 1753

Johnson's Furnace or Iron Works and Bloomsbury Forge, Beach Glen Brook, Morris County, 1751

Kingwood Forges, Lockatoney Creek, Hunterdon County, 1762

Lisbon or New Lisbon Forge, Rancocas Creek, Burlington County, 1730

Little Falls Forge or Gray's Iron Works, Passaic River, Little Falls, Passaic County, 1771

Long Pond Furnace and Forges, near Greenwood Lake, Passaic County, 1768

Lower or North Phoenix Forge, on Honion Lake near Lakehurst, Ocean County, 1816

Martha Furnace, Oswego River, Burlington County, 1793

Middle or Etna Forge, Burnt Meadow branch of Rockaway River, Morris County, 1749

Monmouth Furnace and Williamsburg Forge or Howell Works, Manasquan River, near Freehold in Monmouth County, 1770

Mount Holly Iron Works, Rancocas Creek, Burlington County, 1730

Mount Hope Furnace, Rockaway Township near Dover, Morris County, 1773

Mount Pleasant Forge, Rockaway River, near Morristown, Morris County, 1756

New Mills or Pemberton Forge, Pemberton, Burlington County, 1787

Norton Forge, Muthockawny Creek, Hunterdon County, 1767

Oxford Furnace, branch of Pequest Creek, Warren County, 1742

Pompton Forge and Furnace, Pompton, Passaic County, 1726

Ringwood Furnace and Forges, north branch Pequannock River, Passaic County, 1739

Sharpsborough or Sharpsbury Furnace and Forge, branch of Wallkill River, Sussex County, 1768

Shrewsbury or Monmouth Forge, Shrewsbury River, Monmouth County, 1674

Sparta Forges, at head of Wallkill River, Sussex County, 1785

Speedwell Furnace, east branch of Wading River, Burlington County, 1784

Speedwell Iron Works, Whippany River, Morris County, 1773

Split Rock Bloomery or Dixson's Forge, Beaver Lake, Morris County, 1790

Spotswood Forges, Manolopan River, Middlesex County, 1750

Squire's Point Forge, near source of Musconetcong River, Sussex County, 1760

Stanhope Forges and Furnaces, Musconetcong River, Sussex County, 1780–1800

Sterling Iron Works, in northern Bergen County, now Orange County, N. Y., 1751

Tintern Furnace, Haines' Creek, Burlington County, 1766

Trenton Forge or Iron Works, near Assunpink Creek, Mercer County, 1729

Union Works or Forge, on branch of Wading River, Burlington County, 1802

Union Iron Works and High Bridge or Solitare Forge, near High Bridge on Smalley's Creek, Hunterdon County, 1753

Vesuvius Furnace, Newark, Essex County, 1769

Washington Furnace or Bergen Iron Works, Metedeconk River, Ocean County, 1832

Westecunk, West Creek or Stafford Forge, on north branch of West Creek, Ocean County, 1797

Weymouth Furnace, on Great Egg Harbor River, Atlantic County, 1800

Whippany Bloomery, on Whippany River, Morris County, 1707

Wright's or Federal Forge and Furnace or Dover or Manchester Furnace, on branch of Toms River, Ocean County, 1789

9. WEAVERS

Beach, Josiah, Newark, Essex Co., 1796
Clever, John, Hunterdon Co., 1840
Conger, Samuel, Newark, Essex Co., 1796
Happaugh, Mary, Hunterdon Co., 1842

Lincoln, John, Monmouth Co., 1725
Setzer, Jacob, Sussex Co., 1848
Stiff, John, Stillwater, Sussex Co., 1836
Van Doren, George W., Somerset Co., 1836
Vliet, John, Six-Mile-Run, Somerset Co., 1745
Winans, John, Elizabethtown, Union Co., 1745
Young, Nathaniel, Bergen (Jersey City), Hudson Co., 1838

Bibliography

The Antiquarian, 1929.

Antiques Magazine, 1938.

Barber, John, and Howe, Ward H. *Historical Collections of the State of New Jersey*. New York: S. Tuttle, 1844.

Boyer, Charles S. *Old Inns and Taverns in West Jersey*. Camden: Camden County Historical Society, 1962.

Cooper, Howard M. *History of Camden*. Camden, 1910.

Drepperd, Carl W. *Primer of American Antiques*. Garden City, L. I.: Garden City Publishing Co., 1944

De Halve Maen. The Holland Society of N.Y. Inc., NYC. 1885-1957.

Franklin, Benjamin. *Autobiography*.

Glenney, Walter L. *Historic Roadsides in New Jersey*. Plainfield, N. J.: Society of Colonial Wars, 1928.

Gordon, Thomas F. *History and Gazetteer of New Jersey*. Trenton: David Penton, 1834.

Hatfield, The Reverend. *History of Elizabethtown*. Elizabeth, N. J.: *Daily Journal*, 1876.

Lee, Francis B. *New Jersey, Colony and State*. Trenton, 1875.

Library of Rutgers University, New Brunswick.

Library of The New Jersey Historical Society, Newark.

Mahoney, Joseph H. *New Jersey History Quarterly*. Newark, N. J.: Historical Society.

McKearin, George S., and McKearin, Helen. *American Glass*. New York: Crown Publishers Co., Inc., 1941.

Melick, Andrew. *The Story of an Old Farm.* Somerville, N. J.: *Unionist-Gazette,* 1898.

Nutting, Wallace. *The Clock Book.* Garden City, L. I.: Garden City Publishing Co., 1924.

Ormsbee, Thomas H. *The Story of American Furniture.* New York: The Macmillan Co., 1937.

Parsons, Floyd W. *New Jersey.* Newark, N. J.: New Jersey State Chamber of Commerce, 1928.

Peto, Florence. *Historic Quilts.* New York: The American Historical Co., Inc., 1939.

Salter. *History of Monmouth and Ocean Counties.* Newark, 1898.

Schermerhorn. *The History of Burlington, N. J.* 1880.

Shackleton, Robert, and Shackleton, Elizabeth. *The Quest of the Colonial.* New York: The Century Co., 1907.

Sheperd, Charles E. *History of Gloucester, Cumberland and Salem Counties.* Philadelphia, 1879.

Smith. *History of New Jersey.* n.d.

Stockton, Frank R. *Stories of New Jersey.* New York: American Book Co., 1896.

Van Winkle, Daniel. *History of Bergen County, N. J., from 1630 to 1922.* Jersey City, 1922.

Williamson, Scott Graham. *The American Craftsman.* New York: Bramhall House, 1932.

Woodress, James. *Yankee's Odyssey.* Philadelphia: J. B. Lippincott, 1958.

Wyler, Seymour B. *Old Silver.* New York: Crown Publishers Co., Inc., 1937.

Index

DATE DUE